FOOTPRINTS OF THE MESSENGER ﷺ OF ALLAH

ZULFIQAR RAJA

Table of Contents

ACKNOWLEDGEMENTS 5
ISLAMIC EXPRESSIONS AND REFERENCES 6
PREFACE 9
INTRODUCTION 11
PART I – THE PROPHETIC LIFE 15
Introduction 16
Al Ameen 17
Bahira 22
First Revelations 24
Year of Sorrow 27
Miraaj un'Nabi 28
Hijrah 32
Badr 35
Uhud 37
The Growth of Islam 39
Hudaybiyah 42
Al Fath – The Victory 49
Separation from the Messenger ﷺ of Allah 53
Ever-lasting Legacy 56
Excellence of the Messenger ﷺ of Allah 59
PART II – THE PROPHETIC ATTRIBUTES 63
Introduction 64
The Beauty of the Messenger ﷺ of Allah 67

The Pleasant Scent of the Messenger ﷺ of Allah 71
The Lineage of the Messenger ﷺ of Allah 73
The Humility of the Messenger ﷺ of Allah 76
The Sublime Manner of the Messenger ﷺ of Allah 81
The Food of the Messenger ﷺ of Allah 87
The Dress of the Messenger ﷺ of Allah 91
The Speech of the Messenger ﷺ of Allah 95
The Intellect of the Messenger ﷺ of Allah 100
The Courage of the Messenger ﷺ of Allah 102
The Strength of the Messenger ﷺ of Allah 104
PART III – The PROPHETIC CHARACTER 106
Introduction 107
The Mercy of the Messenger ﷺ of Allah 110
The Generosity of the Messenger ﷺ of Allah 117
The Modesty of the Messenger ﷺ of Allah 122
The Patience of the Messenger ﷺ of Allah 125
The Justice of the Messenger ﷺ of Allah 129
The Perfect conduct of the Messenger ﷺ of Allah 133
The Worship of the Messenger ﷺ of Allah 143
Hadith of Sayyidina Imam Hasan ibn Ali (As) from ibn Abi Hala 153
PART IV – THE PROPHETIC REALITY 163
Introduction 164

The Muhammadan ﷺ Reality 166
The Presence of the Messenger ﷺ of Allah 170
AUTHOR'S NOTE 172
REFERENCES 173
YA SAYYIDI SERIES 177

ACKNOWLEDGEMENTS

Footprints of the Messenger ﷺ of Allah

Copyright © Zulfiqar Raja. 2020. All Rights Reserved.
Registered with Copyright House

Cover Photo. Free Google Images.

All Rights Reserved.

No part of this publication may be reproduced as a whole or in part, stored in a retrieval system, transmitted, in any form or by any means, without prior permission in writing of the author, nor be otherwise circulated in any form of binding or cover other than that in which it is published and without a similar condition including this condition being imposed on the subsequent purchaser.

ISBN: 9798678744036

Dedicated to my late father. May Allah (SWT) Grant him the Highest Ranks of Al Jannah.

ISLAMIC EXPRESSIONS AND REFERENCES

Praising ALLAH

Subhan hu wa ta'Ala. (Glorious is He the High)

Abbreviated (SWT)

When mentioning Sayyidina Muhammad'ur Rasulullah;

ﷺ Salla lahu alayhi wa'ale hi Wasallam.

(May Allah (SWT) Send Blessings and Peace upon him and his family)

When mentioning any of the Prophets of Allah;

Alayhi Salaam. (Peace be upon him)

Abbreviated (AS)

When mentioning a male companion or male member of the blessed household of the Messenger ﷺ of Allah;

RadiyAllahu Anhu. (May Allah be Pleased with him)

Abbreviated (RA)

When mentioning a female companion or a female member of the blessed household of the Messenger ﷺ of Allah;

RadiyAllahu Anha. (May Allah be Pleased with her)

Abbreviated (RA)

When mentioning anyone among the pious scholars, saints and Imams;

Rahmatullah Alayh. (May Allah Bestow peace on him)

Abbreviated (Rh)

Compilers of Sahih Ahadith (Books of hadith)

Scholars of Ahadith have confirmed what the actual Sunnah means. The Sunnah is the 'Path'
of Sayyidina Rasulullah ﷺ (Salla lahu alayhi wa'ale hi Wasallam) and includes his ﷺ every;
word / teaching / action / physical appearance / approval / dis-approval.

Authentic books of Ahadith (plural of hadith);

Book   Author

Sahih Bukhari – (Imam Bukhari (Rh))
Sahih Muslim – (Imam Muslim (Rh))
Sunan Abu Daawud – (Imam Abu Daawud (Rh))
Musnad Ahmed – (Imam Ahmed bin Hanbal (Rh))
Sunan ibn Majah – (Imam ibn Majah (Rh))
Jaami Tirmidhi / Ashaam-il – (Imam Tirmidhi (Rh))
Sunan An-Nasai – (Imam Nasai (Rh))

(Rh) – Rahmatullah Alayh

Schools of Islamic Sharia and Fiqh

Hanafi – (Imam Abu Hanifa (Rh))
Maaliki – (Imam Maalik (Rh))
Shaaf'I – (Imam Shaafee (Rh))
Hanbali – (Imam Ahmed Ibn Hanbal (Rh))

(Rh) – Rahmatullah Alayh

PREFACE

Bismillah Hir'Rahman Nir'Rahim

(Allah's Name I begin with, The Kind, The Merciful).

Allah Humma Sali Ala' Sayyidina Muhammadin wa'ala Ale' hi Sayyidina Muhammadin, qad dha'ataq, Heelati Adrikni Ya Rasulullah ﷺ

(O' Allah, Raise our Master Muhammad ﷺ. and his ﷺ Family, I cannot find my way out of my plight, remove me from this. Reach me O' Messenger ﷺ of Allah).

---

*'I wept bitterly one night before God and asked Him:
Why is the Muslim so miserable?
Came the reply, 'Don't you know,
this Community possesses the heart but has no beloved'.*

*(Allamah Muhammad Iqbal, 'Armaghan-i Hijaz'
(1938))*

As I lay awake one night, reciting *Salawat* upon Sayyidina Rasulullah ﷺ (Salla lahu alayhi wa'ale hi Wasallam), I realized how my mind had been wandering to places afar, yet I was in the pretence that I was in Medina t'ul Munnawarah. This was the tragedy that has engulfed me, and many worshippers who are present in body when praying long nights, yet absent in soul. They allow the shells of themselves to sit attentively in Allah's Presence, yet their inner selves are long asleep. We rejoice at the belief that we are Muslims, we prostrate to our Lord, and think we are following in the footsteps of our beloved Messenger ﷺ. We attend gatherings, wearing our best garments, after applying perfume and recite loudly, in order that others can admire our dedication. Yet these gatherings have rid us of our anonymity, we seek the recognition of others, and yet fail to please our Lord. Then many years, and thousands of prayers later, we ask why our prayers failed to change our state. This question brought me to this brief interlude with my own faith.

Zulfiqar Raja

INTRODUCTION

A name that remains when all before has passed, is the name of Muhammad ﷺ Ibn Abdullah. This is the blessed name of the Final Messenger; the Seal of Prophethood; the Last Soul to receive Divine Revelation; the one with whom all Guidance and Inspiration passes through; the Master of Men and Jinn; Sayyidina Muhammad ﷺ' ur Rasulullah.

This is a brief account discussing the attributes and qualities of Sayyidina Rasulullah ﷺ (Salla lahu alayhi wa'ale hi Wasallam), supported by authentic texts, while recognising the fact that all texts compiled by man have failed to elaborate upon the magnificence of a Prophet, who was created as a man, yet stood in the Divine Presence of his ﷺ Lord. The Lord Who Continues to Bestow upon His Beloved ﷺ, all apparent and hidden jewels of excellence. This work is a humble note to my Master, my message to Sayyidina Rasulullah ﷺ (Salla lahu alayhi wa'ale hi Wasallam), as I remind myself, of where I had failed in recognizing the attributes of the name I recite when reciting the *Kalima*, in which Allah (SWT) Orders us to bear witness, that Allah (SWT) Is the Only One Worthy of Worship; and Muhammad ﷺ is the Messenger of Allah.

Allah (SWT) States in His Noble Qur'an;

'Did We not Exalt you in your Fame'. (94:4)

I have always been fascinated how Sayyidina Rasulullah ﷺ (Salla lahu alayhi wa'ale hi Wasallam), came into this world, clothed in the unique qualities, which were seen in the previous Prophets of Allah, on whom May Allah (SWT) Bestow Peace. The Prophetic life of Sayyidina

Rasulullah ﷺ (Salla lahu alayhi wa'ale hi Wasallam) with all his ﷺ characteristics became its own proof of Prophethood, even before revelation of his ﷺ miracles. The name of Sayyidina Rasulullah ﷺ (Salla lahu alayhi wa'ale hi Wasallam), went far and wide through many different lands, and caused kings, tribal leaders and humble dwellers alike to travel to meet him ﷺ. The stories of Sayyidina Abu Dharr Ghafari (RadiyAllahu Anhu) who endured great hardship upon his journey to meet Sayyidina Rasulullah ﷺ (Salla lahu alayhi wa'ale hi Wasallam), which culminated in severe beatings from the people of Makka, after he declared the *Kalima* openly, more so in ecstasy of the person who he had just pledged allegiance to, rather than the faith he had just found. We have read about the *'Persian'*; Sayyidina Salman Farsi (RadiyAllahu Anhu) who travelled to the *'Land of Palm Trees'*, where his studies informed him would be the place the Final Messenger ﷺ would appear. Sayyidina Salman Farsi (RadiyAllahu Anhu) was enslaved en route, a fate he readily accepted as long as it brought him to the feet of the *Seal of all Messengers*. Later, Sayyidina Salman Farsi (RadiyAllahu Anhu) was awarded his freedom after finally meeting the Messenger ﷺ of Allah.

The companions (RadiyAllahu Anhumma) had never experienced a religion like Islam, the faith brought with the Message of Sayyidina Rasulullah ﷺ (Salla lahu alayhi wa'ale hi Wasallam). This was not just a faith based on worship, and devotion, this was a faith of humanity. A religion that taught principles of serving the common man, protecting the weak, and self-sacrificing in love for the neighbour. The faith of Islam was not just based on the Divine Book, the like of which had been partly revealed before. This was a religion that stood tall on the shoulders of a man, someone of the Arab community, who had mercy and compassion, despite being brought up in a harsh environment where burying baby daughters alive was prevalent in local traditions. Killing over tribal differences, fornication, indulging in intoxicants, immorality, and the buying and selling of slaves was widely practiced. Yet this man, a young man who was orphaned at a young age, who had no formal education, possessed the best of morals. This was the greatest proof that Sayyidina Muhammad ﷺ could not be like any other, how can an orphan in a society that was led by men proud of their forefathers, become the most respected and trusted? How can a man who had never ventured out to other lands, have the intellect to confound the most literate men of his ﷺ time, and possessed the knowledge of previous texts? This was a man who broke away from the inhuman traditions of society, and was revered by his companions (RadiyAllahu Anhumma), and enemies alike. The legacy of Sayyidina Rasulullah ﷺ (Salla lahu alayhi wa'ale hi Wasallam), has transcended every test of time, and even today, generations are inspired by the life of Sayyidina Rasulullah ﷺ (Salla lahu alayhi wa'ale hi Wasallam).

This work includes the; *'Prophetic Life'*; *'Prophetic Attributes'*; and *'Prophetic Character'*, before culminating into the final section; *'Prophetic Reality'*, which is the *core* of the fruit of this treatise. Included in this work are verses from the Noble Qur'an, with extensive accounts from the authentic ahadith, which also include insight from the pen of the true scholars of Islam.

A man once read the text of the great Muslim scholar and philosopher; *'Muhammad Iqbal'*, May Allah (SWT) Have Mercy on him, who wrote that even if you deny Allah (SWT) as atheists do, by claiming that they cannot believe in the Unseen, yet how can you deny Prophet Muhammad ﷺ? A Prophet who brought the greatest revolution despite having the most modest of means, and conquered his ﷺ land, from where they exiled him ﷺ, without shedding a single drop of blood. This was after nations had surrendered their hearts and will to him ﷺ, after abandoning their ancient pagan beliefs. The Messenger ﷺ of Allah brought a religion for the common man to follow, which brought King and Slave together, to prostrate to the same Lord. Yet they knew that the Messenger ﷺ was not like them, they witnessed him ﷺ splitting the moon; experienced fountains of water gushing out from his ﷺ blessed fingers, and the sun being halted at his ﷺ command. Sayyidina Rasulullah ﷺ (Salla lahu alayhi wa'ale hi Wasallam), is the best of mankind, yet chose to live in poverty, among the most humble of his ﷺ community, in the words of Iqbal (Rh), the Messenger ﷺ of Allah was *'content when people were not even patient, was merciful when others were not even just'.* This man accepted Islam, reading this text of Allamah Muhammad Iqbal (Rh), who quite simply said the greatest proof of Islam, is the Messenger ﷺ of Allah.

In *Rumuz-i Bekhudi,* first published in 1918, Iqbal (Rh) speaks of the role of Prophethood in the life of the community. *"God fashioned forth our form,"* he says, *"and through Apostleship breathed in our flesh the soul of life. . . . [It] shaped our being, gave us Faith and Law, converted our vast myriads into one, and joined our fractions in a mighty whole inseparable, indivisible. . . His* ﷺ *was the breath that gave the people life; his sun shone glory on their risen dawn. In God the Individual, in him* [i.e. Sayyidina Muhammad ﷺ (Salla lahu alayhi wa'ale hi Wasallam] *lives the Community, in his* ﷺ *sun's rays resplendent ever; his* ﷺ *Apostleship brought concord to our purpose and our goal."*

PART I – THE PROPHETIC LIFE

Introduction

The blessed life of Sayyidina Rasulullah ﷺ (Salla lahu alayhi wa'ale hi Wasallam) is an essential study for all Muslims along with studying 'Al'Qur'an' and the books of authentic Ahadith. The exemplary conduct, habits, actions, characteristics, trials, tests and ultimate victory of the Messenger ﷺ of Allah, are viewed as miraculous and the undeniable evidence of how 'Al'Qur'an' has a living form.

The authentic books of *Seerah,* which explain and present the life of Sayyidina Rasulullah ﷺ (Salla lahu alayhi wa'ale hi Wasallam) demonstrate how the blessed Messenger ﷺ had such a birth that *nur* – light descended with him ﷺ from inside his ﷺ blessed mother; Sayyidina Amina bint Wahb (Alayhi Salaam). The Messenger ﷺ of Allah, did not have an umbilical cord attached. The sustenance given to the Messenger ﷺ of Allah, who is the 'Best of all Creation', came from Allah (SWT) directly. Sayyidina Rasulullah ﷺ (Salla lahu alayhi wa'ale hi Wasallam) descended into this world already in a state of circumcision and therefore no being ever saw the most blessed of all creation in an uncovered state. (Al Mawahib)

Sheikh Ibn Taymeeyah (Rh) mentioned the qualities of Sayyidina Rasulullah ﷺ (Salla lahu alayhi wa'ale hi wasallam) in his work, titled, *'Jawab as-Sahih Liman badala din al-Masih'*. This book included many evidences of the unparalleled excellence of the life of the *'Seal of all Messengers'*. Some parts of the book have been used in the below summary. References are also taken from the great work of *'Kitab'Ash-Shifa'* by Imam Qadi Iyad (Rh) and *'Al Mawahib al-Laduniyya'* by Imam Qastallani (Rh). The great text of Shaykh Ibn Ata'Illah As-Sakandary (Rh) has also been used for further understanding of Qur'anic verses, from his priceless work *'Al Kitab at'Tanwir'*.

Al Ameen

And Verily, you (O Muhammad ﷺ) are on an exalted standard of character.

(Al' Qur'an; 68,4)

Sayyidina Rasulullah ﷺ (Salla lahu alayhi wa'ale hi Wasallam) is a direct descendant from the Father of all Prophets; Sayyidina Ibrahim (Alayhi Salaam) - *Abraham*, to whose descendants Allah (SWT) bestowed the Book and the *Sunnah*. All the Prophets and Messengers, Peace be upon them, to come after Sayyidina Ibrahim (Alayhi Salaam) came from his blessed family, through the lineage of his two sons: Sayyidina Isma'il (As) – *Ishmael* and Sayyidina Ishaq (As) - *Isaac*.

The 'Torah' mentions the merits of the offspring of Sayyidina Isma'il (As), their reference and eligibility belongs to Sayyidina Muhammad ﷺ'ur Rasulullah (Salla lahu alayhi wa'ale hi Wasallam). After the building of *Baitullah* Kaaba, by Sayyidina Ibrahim (Alayhi Salaam) along with his elder son; Sayyidina Isma'il (Alayhi Salaam), he prayed to Allah (SWT) for four things as his reward. The first was to make Makkah a city of security; the second to bless the fruits of this blessed city; the third that from *their* offspring, through the lineage of his son Sayyidina Isma'il (Alayhi Salaam); there will always be a group of believers who remain on the path of *Tauheed* – La illaha il-Allah *(There is no god but Allah)*. This supplication of Sayyidina Ibrahim (Alayhi Salaam) culminated in asking for the coming of the Final Messenger ﷺ, who would bring the blessed Book; the *Ayaat* – Verses; and would purify the believers. This supplication was for the coming of

Sayyidina Rasulullah ﷺ (Salla lahu alayhi wa'ale hi Wasallam), and the nation who would always remain on the path of Islamic Monotheism.

Our Lord! Send amongst them a Messenger of their own, who shall recite unto them Your verses and instruct them in the Book and wisdom, and sanctify them, Verily! You are the All- Mighty, the All Wise.

(Al' Qur'an; 2:129)

That group who would come from the lineage of Sayyidina Ibrahim (Alayhi Salaam), and his son; Sayyidina Isma'il (Alayhi Salaam) would be the ancestors of Sayyidina Muhammad ﷺ'ur Rasulullah (Salla lahu alayhi wa'ale hi Wasallam). There were no traditions of the *Jahiliyyah* – period of ignorance, such as idol worship or fornication found in the ancestry of Sayyidina Rasulullah ﷺ (Salla lahu alayhi wa'ale hi Wasallam). The Noble Messenger ﷺ of Allah came from the most blessed loins, passing through the most honourable of people who practised the true religion of Allah (SWT).

Of the family of Sayyidina Ibrahim (As), the Quraysh are the most respected and honoured, from the Quraysh, it is the tribe of Banu Hashim who are regarded as their best offspring. Sayyidina Rasulullah ﷺ (Salla lahu alayhi wa'ale hi Wasallam) is the best of the sons of Banu Hashim. This has been narrated in an authentic hadith; *'Allah (SWT) divided the creation into two groups, the light of the Messenger ﷺ of Allah (Salla lahu alayhi wa'ale hi Wasallam) was placed into the lineage of the best group among them'*. (Kitab' Ash-Shifa)

Sayyidina Rasulullah ﷺ (Salla lahu alayhi wa'ale hi Wasallam) came into this world in the city of Makka t'ul Makkaramah. This blessed city is the mother of all cities as situated within it is 'Baitullah' Kaaba. Its foundation was placed by Sayyidina Adam (Alayhi Salaam) - *Adam*. and was later built by Sayyidina Ibrahim (As) and Sayyidina Isma'il (As) for the sole Worship of Allah (SWT). After which Sayyidina Ibrahim (As) called all the believers from then up to the end of time, to travel to this city, and perform the pilgrimage. Since that time, the holy pilgrimage is being performed by believers, and this is mentioned in every scripture. The Messenger ﷺ of Allah was selected to descend into this world in the city that was established as the focal point in the Worship of Allah (SWT).

On the night when Sayyidina Rasulullah ﷺ (Salla lahu alayhi wa'ale hi Wasallam) descended, it is thought to be the year 570 AD, in the month of Rabi'ul Awwal. This was the manifestation of the Final Messenger ﷺ (Salla lahu alayhi wa'ale hi Wasallam), not the birth or creation of him ﷺ. Books of Islamic literature mention from narrations that Sayyidina Rasulullah ﷺ (Salla lahu alayhi wa'ale hi Wasallam) was created before the first man; Sayyidina Adam (Alayhi Salaam) - *Adam*, in the form of pure light, this light remained in the Hand of Allah (SWT), worshipping the Divine Creator for two thousand years. (Kitab'Ash-Shifa).

The night of the *'Mawlid'*, was a night of countless miracles, witnessed in the heavens and earth. The blessed mother of Sayyidina Rasulullah ﷺ (Salla lahu alayhi wa'ale hi Wasallam); Sayyidina Amina bint Wahb (Alayhi Salaam) was visited by two blessed ladies who were; Sayyidina Maryam (Alayhi Salaam) – *Virgin Mary*; and Sayyidina Asiya (Alayhi Salaam) - *Asiyah*. As Sayyidina Amina (Alayhi Salaam) felt thirsty she was given a drink from the heavens, which was as white as milk and as sweet as honey. SubhanAllah. (Al Mawaahib Sharif)

On the night of the descent into this world of the Messenger ﷺ of Allah, the gates of Paradise were opened, flags were raised on the Blessed Kaaba, and flags could be seen in the East and West. The idols of the Pagans, fell in prostration and the Kaaba spoke, proclaiming *'Allah Ho Akbar'*- Allah is Great. The East and West were illuminated, and the palaces in Syria and Rome shook. (Sirah al 'Nabi). These are few of the many miracles of that magnificent moment detailed in books of *Seerah*, of when Sayyidina Rasulullah ﷺ (Salla lahu alayhi wa'ale hi

Wasallam), the Seal of All Prophets and Messengers, arrived as the *Rahmat al' Alameen* – Mercy onto the Worlds.

Allah (SWT) mentions that Sayyidina Rasulullah ﷺ (Salla lahu alayhi wa'ale hi Wasallam) came from *'among yourselves'* (9:128), meaning that the Messenger ﷺ of Allah came from within the people so that they would know him ﷺ and his ﷺ qualities, witness his ﷺ truthfulness and be assured of his ﷺ blessed rank. Allah (SWT) introduced mankind to His own Attributes through the sending of the Final Messenger ﷺ (Salla lahu alayhi wa'ale hi Wasallam), even bestowing on him ﷺ two of His Own qualities of being 'compassionate' – *Ra'uf*, ', and 'merciful' – *Rahim*. Sayyidina Rasulullah ﷺ (Salla lahu alayhi wa'ale hi Wasallam) has been mentioned in the Noble Qur'an of having these qualities. These qualities were apparent so that the people would recognise the Messenger ﷺ of Allah as one of their own.

The Messenger ﷺ of Allah, was from the blessed city but was raised in the rural area outside of Makka t'ul Makkaramah. Sayyidina Rasulullah ﷺ (Salla lahu alayhi wa'ale hi Wasallam) was orphaned at a young age, as his ﷺ blessed father; Sayyidina Abdullah ibn Abdul Muttalib (Alayhi Salaam) passed away before his ﷺ noble birth, and blessed mother also passed away when the Messenger ﷺ of Allah, was only six years of age. However, Sayyidina Rasulullah ﷺ (Salla lahu alayhi wa'ale hi Wasallam) had the best of upbringing, there was no shortcoming in the speech, actions and conduct of the Final Messenger ﷺ (Salla lahu alayhi wa'ale hi Wasallam). The blessed Messenger ﷺ of Allah was 'unlettered', meaning the Messenger ﷺ of Allah did not acquire formal education. This is not the same as being 'illiterate'. It is a grave sin to claim the Messenger ﷺ of Allah was illiterate, as this is a defect, and means to be ignorant of knowledge. There is no defect, or shortcoming in the Messenger ﷺ of Allah. The Messenger ﷺ of Allah has the title of being 'unlettered', which was another evidence of the most elevated rank of the Messenger ﷺ of Allah. It meant that the Final Messenger ﷺ (Salla lahu alayhi wa'ale hi Wasallam) did not have any teacher or mentor, meaning there is no person who could have taught the Best ﷺ of all Messengers (Salla lahu alayhi wa'ale hi Wasallam). To teach a student implies you have greater knowledge than the student, and therefore the teacher has a position of greater respect than the student. However it is not possible for anyone to have held a greater rank than the Messenger ﷺ of Allah, who is *'Khayr-e-Khalqi'*, the best of creation. The knowledge of all things was bestowed upon the blessed heart of Sayyidina Rasulullah ﷺ (Salla lahu alayhi wa'ale hi Wasallam) through Divine Revelation, and Inspiration from Allah (SWT), Who Holds the dominion of all things.

Sayyidina Rasulullah ﷺ (Salla lahu alayhi wa'ale hi Wasallam) was guarded from the environment around him ﷺ, and was not given to lie, to oppress or to indulge in any indecency. The Messenger ﷺ of Allah was known by great titles of respect, which were a reflection of his ﷺ blessed character. These titles were *'Al Ameen'*, which means the trustworthy, and *'Al Saadiq'*, the truthful. Sayyidina Rasulullah ﷺ (Salla lahu alayhi wa'ale hi Wasallam) was known for these qualities, and for his ﷺ justice and mercy towards others. The people of Makka would entrust their possessions with him ﷺ for safekeeping. This was before the revelations came, and before the time when people actually became aware that Sayyidina Muhammad ﷺ ibn Abdullah, is the Messenger ﷺ of Allah. This was further proof that the Messenger ﷺ of Allah has been created without any fault or blemish and descended into this world as the perfect example for mankind to follow. This had become apparent long before the revelations began.

In Mount Hira, approximately in the year 610 AD, the revelations came to the Messenger ﷺ of Allah at forty years of age. Prophet Muhammad ﷺ (Salla lahu alayhi wa'ale hi Wasallam) was created as a Prophet, and was guided as such from the time of entering the world. Even declaring the Prophethood at the time of his ﷺ birth. The Prophets of Allah spent periods of their life before receiving revelations among their people, so that their truth and sublime character became evident, and their message from Allah (SWT) would be accepted. However, as was seen with all the previous nations, they still rejected the Message, despite believing in the truthfulness of the Prophets of Allah.

Bahira

One of the earliest incidents in which the actual rank of the Messenger ﷺ of Allah became known, took place when the Messenger ﷺ of Allah was nine years of age. The Messenger ﷺ was accompanying his ﷺ Uncle and Guardian; Sayyidina Abu Talib, to Syria as part of a business expedition. They passed a monastery on the way where monks resided and would be occupied in devotion and worship. However, on this particular day as the convoy approached, a monk came out and met them, introducing himself as 'Bahira'. This had never happened before. Bahira requested the travellers to be his guests, and Sayyidina Abu Talib accepted the invitation.

When the group sat for the meal, Bahira enquired about the young boy who was with them, and was informed that the boy was outside guarding their possessions. Bahira requested they invite him in at once. This boy was Sayyidina Muhammad ﷺ ibn Abdullah (Salla lahu alayhi wa'ale hi Wasallam). Bahira asked questions about him, about his heritage and guardians. Sayyidina Abu Talib said that this boy was his son. Bahira refused to believe this and Sayyidina Abu Talib explained that he would call him his son, but was really his nephew. The parents of Sayyidina Muhammad ﷺ ibn Abdullah's parents (Salla lahu alayhi wa'ale hi Wasallam) had passed away, and his ﷺ grandfather who had been his ﷺ guardian, had also passed away. Bahira accepted this response. Bahira later approached Abu Talib and informed him that his nephew was actually the Final Prophet, who's coming had been forecasted in the previous scriptures. Bahira knew that the Final Messenger ﷺ (Salla lahu alayhi wa'ale hi Wasallam) would be an orphan and this is why he knew that Sayyidina Abu Talib could not be his ﷺ father. Bahira explained that he saw the signs, when their caravan approached in the distance, and he saw a cloud was shading them. There had been no clouds at all before the caravan arrived. When the caravan stopped under a tree, the cloud had also stopped above them. Bahira said that he had also seen the stones and the trees prostrating as the convoy was passing by. Bahira came out to see this phenomenon, and witnessed that the stones and trees were prostrating to the young Sayyidina Muhammad ﷺ (Salla lahu alayhi wa'ale hi Wasallam), and it was this young boy, who the cloud was shading. Bahira explained that these are the signs mentioned in the Torah, and are only revealed upon a Prophet of Allah. Bahira also checked the blessed back of Sayyidina Muhammad ﷺ ibn Abdullah's (Salla lahu alayhi wa'ale hi Wasallam) blessed back and saw the *'Seal of the Prophets'*, which was an oval shape protruding just below the shoulder blades. This was also one of the signs of the Final Messenger ﷺ (Salla lahu alayhi wa'ale hi Wasallam) described in the previous scriptures. Bahira said *"This is the master of all humans, Allah will send him ﷺ with a message which would be a mercy to all humans"*. Bahira advised that this young boy be taken back to Makka at once, and should not go to Syria, where the Jewish people resided. Bahira feared that if he had recognised this young boy as the Final Messenger ﷺ, then so would the learned among the Jewish community, and they may try to harm him ﷺ. Sayyidina Abu Talib took heed of this advice, and returned with the Messenger ﷺ of Allah back to Makka.

First Revelations

Sayyidina Rasulullah ﷺ (Salla lahu alayhi wa'ale hi Wasallam) received the first revelations of 'Al'Qur'an', in the cave of Hira where the chief of angels, Sayyidina Jibrail (As) brought the revelation to *'Read'*. The arch-angel; Jibrail – *Angel Gabriel*, had previously descended with the revelations to Sayyidina Musa (Alayhi Salaam) – *Moses*, and Sayyidina Eesa (Alayhi Salaam) – *Jesus*.

Sayyidina Rasulullah ﷺ (Salla lahu alayhi wa'ale hi Wasallam) asked upon receiving this first command, 'What shall I read'? *(This account is often mis-represented in books of Seerah, with the Messenger ﷺ of Allah saying the words, 'I cannot read'. This is a gross error, as a Prophet of Allah would not refuse an order received from his Lord, this would be against the etiquette a Prophet would have with Allah (SWT))*.

Sayyidina Jibrail (As) replied *'Read in the name of your Lord'*...... The first verses revealed are found in *'Surah Alaq'*, which is Chapter 96, verses 1-5, of the Noble Qur'an.

The Messenger ﷺ of Allah, was given the weight of the task for which the whole universe had been created, as his ﷺ rank is that of the best of all creation, therefore the ultimate guidance for mankind was to be revealed to him ﷺ.

The noble wife of the Messenger ﷺ of Allah was; Sayyidina Khadijah t'ul Kubraa (RadiyAllahu Anha), who was also the first to accept Islam. Sayyidina Khadijah t'ul Kubraa, May Allah (SWT) Be Pleased with her, was older than the Messenger ﷺ of Allah. She was a wealthy lady, who was known for her business acumen, and was also a widow. Sayyidina Khadijah (RadiyAllahu Anha) proposed to the Messenger ﷺ of Allah, after witnessing his ﷺ honesty in dealing with her business affairs. At the time of the first revelations, she comforted the Messenger ﷺ of Allah, fulfilling the duties of a wife, and showed the regard she had for the character of the Messenger ﷺ of Allah. Sayyidina Khadijah t'ul Kubraa (RadiyAllahu Anha) reassured Sayyidina

Rasulullah ﷺ (Salla lahu alayhi wa'ale hi Wasallam) that Allah (SWT) Will never humiliate him ﷺ, or burden him ﷺ, as the Messenger ﷺ of Allah upholds the truth, treats his ﷺ kin with respect, looks after the travellers, and helps the needy and weak. These beautiful words of support are always mentioned in Islamic literature. A wife knows her husband best, even when the world respects a person, it is a man's wife who truly knows his affairs. Here Sayyidina Khadijah's (RadiyAllahu Anha) kind words for her husband, showed the tremendous respect she had for the Messenger ﷺ of Allah, before she became aware of his ﷺ Prophethood.

Sayyidina Rasulullah ﷺ (Salla lahu alayhi wa'ale hi Wasallam) practised Islam based on the revelations being revealed to him ﷺ, largely in private. Only a few had accepted the religion, these included his ﷺ dear nephew; Sayyidina Ali ibn Abi Talib (Alayhi Salaam); and his ﷺ dear friend, Sayyidina Abu Bakr Siddique (RadiyAllahu Anhu). After three years had passed, Allah (SWT) Ordered His Messenger ﷺ to now openly declare the Message of Islam, and invite all to the true religion. The weak and helpless joined the Messenger ﷺ of Allah, and the most affluent and powerful opposed his ﷺ Divine Message to Believe and Worship Allah (SWT) Alone, and follow him ﷺ, the Final Messenger. This had been predicted by the people of knowledge, foretold by Bahira during the youth of Sayyidina Rasulullah ﷺ (Salla lahu alayhi wa'ale hi Wasallam), and also by Waraqa ibn Nawfal, a Priest, who was the paternal cousin of Sayyidina Khadijah t'ul Kubraa (RadiyAllahu Anha). He had told the Messenger ﷺ of Allah, shortly after the revelations began that the people of Makka will become his ﷺ enemies, and will force him ﷺ out of his ﷺ land, as this happened to all the Prophets of Allah, before him ﷺ. Peace be upon them all.

Those that accepted Islam, and witnessed the blessed countenance of Sayyidina Rasulullah ﷺ, were given the honour of being his ﷺ companions. They were the *Sahaabah* (May Allah (SWT) Be Pleased with them). The blessed household of the Messenger ﷺ of Allah, are called the *'Ahl ul'Bayt'*, Peace be upon them, literally meaning 'People of the house'. They have a unique honour of having the blood lines of the Messenger ﷺ of Allah.

The best amongst people were chosen to accompany the Messenger ﷺ of Allah. The first female to become a believer was Sayyidina Khadijah t'ul Kubraa (RadiyAllahu Anha), who was also the first to pray behind the Messenger ﷺ of Allah. (Ibn Kathir). The first grown male to accept Islam on the blessed hand of Sayyidina Rasulullah ﷺ (Salla lahu alayhi wa'ale hi Wasallam) was his ﷺ faithful friend; Sayyidina Abu Bakr Siddique (RadiyAllahu Anhu), and the first child was the young cousin of the Messenger ﷺ of Allah, and the son of Sayyidina Abu Talib; Sayyidina Ali ibn Abi Talib (RadiyAllahu Anhu). Later, even the fiercest enemies of Islam became the defenders of the faith, upon hearing the Divine Message, men who were feared like Sayyidina Umar ibn Khattab (RadiyAllahu Anhu). Umar was given the title of *'Al Farooq'*, the one who separates the truth from falsehood. Originally, Umar had been an ardent enemy of Islam, and one day set out to harm the Messenger ﷺ of Allah. On the way, he was told that his own sister and her husband had accepted Islam. In a state of rage, Umar changed direction and made his way to his sister's house, upon entering he found his sister reciting verses from the Noble Qur'an. Umar Ibn Khattab began to beat his sister and also struck her husband. But he was astounded as a man who was feared by all, found that his own sister was now unafraid and continued to declare her faith in Islam. This moved him, and he demanded to see the text that she was reciting. He was told that to touch the Noble Book, he would need to purify himself first, which he agreed to do. Umar Ibn Khattab, performed ablution, and sat down to recite the verses of the Noble Qur'an, which had transformed his younger sister. He recited verses from *'Surah Ta-Ha'*, and wept uncontrollably, as his heart opened to the Divine truth. Umar Ibn Khattab set out to the humble dwellings of Sayyidina Rasulullah ﷺ (Salla lahu alayhi wa'ale hi Wasallam) and when asked upon his arrival of whether he came to threaten the blessed life of the Messenger ﷺ of Allah, which he had previously vowed to do. He replied that in fact he had come to give his own life into the hands of the Final Messenger ﷺ.

Year of Sorrow

The Companions of the Messenger ﷺ of Allah, stood firm in the face of persecution and stood by the side of the Messenger ﷺ of Allah despite being ostracized, and violently attacked. The most severe treatment was endured by Sayyidina Rasulullah ﷺ (Salla lahu alayhi wa'ale hi Wasallam) himself. Even after some of the companions began to migrate to other lands, as ordered by him ﷺ, the Messenger ﷺ of Allah stayed in Makka with some of his ﷺ closest companions. The Messenger ﷺ of Allah also suffered a great loss when his ﷺ faithful wife passed away, and also lost another great supporter in his Uncle; Abu Talib, who also passed away. This was known as the 'Year of Sorrow'. It was the most testing time for Sayyidina Rasulullah ﷺ (Salla lahu alayhi wa'ale hi Wasallam), and the tribulations were further heightened when the Messenger ﷺ of Allah visited Taif. This was a small town, on the outskirts of Makka Sharif. It was in this small town that the residents hurled stones and abuse at the most Elevated ﷺ of all Messengers (Salla lahu alayhi wa'ale hi Wasallam), after rejecting his ﷺ message. Bloodied and in tears, Sayyidina Rasulullah ﷺ (Salla lahu alayhi wa'ale hi Wasallam) left this town, and sought refuge under a tree. Allah (SWT) Ordered His angels to comfort him ﷺ and the angels asked his ﷺ permission to crush the people of Taif for their insolence. Sayyidina Rasulullah ﷺ (Salla lahu alayhi wa'ale hi Wasallam) who was sent as a mercy upon the worlds, *'Rahmat lil' Alameen'*, pardoned them, saying that if not them then their offspring will accept the religion of Islam.

Miraaj un'Nabi

'Glory be to Him who carried His slave by night from the Masjid al-Haram to the Masjid Al-Aqsa, the vicinity of which we have blessed, to show him some of Our signs. He is the Hearing, the Seeing'. (Al Qur'an; 17:1)

Sayyidina Rasulullah ﷺ (Salla lahu alayhi wa'ale hi Wasallam) ascended to the greatest of heights where no being had gone before spiritually or physically, on the Night of *'Al Isra' Wal Miraj'*. This night remains the most miraculous journey in which Allah (SWT) called upon His most beloved Messenger ﷺ (Salla lahu alayhi wa'ale hi Wasallam) to His Divine Presence. The above verse from the Noble Qur'an, mentions that Allah (SWT) called His Slave to travel from the Harem of Makka t'ul Makkaramah to the blessed sanctuary of Masjid Al Aqsa, in Jerusalem. Allah (SWT) Mentions the Messenger ﷺ of Allah as His 'slave' in this verse, because when Allah (SWT) Calls upon His Messenger, it will be as His *'Slave'*, and when He sends him ﷺ, it will be as His *'Messenger'*.

Sayyidina Rasulullah ﷺ (Salla lahu alayhi wa'ale hi Wasallam) was sleeping in the *Harem* of the Kaaba in Makka, when Sayyidina Jibrail (Alayhi Salaam), the Chief of the Angels, woke him ﷺ. This can be understood as getting the attention of the Messenger ﷺ of Allah, as when the eyes of the Prophets sleep, their hearts remain awake.

The blessed chest of the Messenger ﷺ of Allah was split open and Sayyidina Jibrail (As), the chief of the angels, brought a basin, removing the internal organs of the Messenger ﷺ of Allah, washing them with the purest of water, and then pouring inside the blessed chest of the Messenger ﷺ, the wonders of all creation, courage and wisdom. The blessed chest of Sayyidina Rasulullah ﷺ (Salla lahu alayhi wa'ale hi Wasallam) was then sealed. This had been done on several occasions in the life of the Messenger ﷺ of Allah, and there is difference of opinion of whether this was also done on this miraculous night. Here is the proof that the Messenger ﷺ of Allah was in fact a; *Bashar* – human being, and *Nur* – pure light. This miracle resembles the creation of the forefather of mankind, Sayyidina Adam (Alayhi Salaam) whose creation was miraculous. The human attribute of the Messenger ﷺ of Allah, was the splitting of his ﷺ blessed chest, and the attribute of being pure light, is what allowed him ﷺ to have the lights of certainty poured within.

Sayyidina Jibrail (Alayhi Salaam) brought the conveyance for the journey, a heavenly animal, called the *'Buraq'*. It was brought bridled and saddled to the Messenger ﷺ of Allah on this evening, whereas the Buraq had been ridden bareback by the preceding Prophets of Allah, Peace be upon them. The Buraq shied away from the Messenger ﷺ of Allah, and Sayyidina Jibrail (As) took the reins of the animal, and said 'Do you do this to Sayyidina Muhammad ﷺ, no one more honoured by Allah (SWT), has ever ridden you'. The *Buraq* broke into a sweat upon hearing this. (Ash-Shifa)

Sayyidina Rasulullah ﷺ (Salla lahu alayhi wa'ale hi Wasallam) mounted the Buraq and was taken from the sanctuary of the Harem in Makka t'ul Makkaramah, to the blessed sanctuary of Masjid Al Aqsa, in Jerusalem. There the most blessed congregation was assembled, as all the Prophets of Allah, May Peace be upon them all, were led in prayer by, the Final Messenger ﷺ, who is the Seal of all Prophets (As), and the Leader of the Prophets, Peace be unto them. Sayyidina Rasulullah ﷺ (Salla lahu alayhi wa'ale hi Wasallam) had completed the first part of this miraculous night, which was *'Al Israa'*- the journey.

From this sanctuary, the *'Miraaj'* also took place. This is the 'Ascent' of the Messenger ﷺ of Allah on the heavenly ladder, to the greater heavens, in body, mind and spirit. This was the greatest honour bestowed upon man, as Sayyidina Rasulullah ﷺ, ascended past all known limits, to be in the Presence of the Creator. The Messenger ﷺ of

Allah, witnessed the wonders of creation through this night, as well as conversing with certain Prophets of Allah, Peace be upon them.

Sayyidina Rasulullah ﷺ (Salla lahu alayhi wa'ale hi Wasallam) then ascended past the point from which nothing had ever passed. Even the limits of Sayyidina Jibrail (As) ended here. This is *'Sidra t'ul Muntaha'*, where the Lote tree is situated, and nothing is known beyond this point, except what exists in the Divine Knowledge of Allah (SWT), some of which was Bestowed upon the Messenger ﷺ of Allah.

Allah (SWT) Directly Conversed with the Messenger ﷺ of Allah, and then Granted the Messenger ﷺ of Allah, even greater bounties. This included the *Salaah* - the prayers to be performed, reduced from fifty to five, on the insistence of Sayyidina Musa (Alayhi Salaam); *Moses*, who would repeatedly send the Messenger ﷺ to Allah (SWT) for greater concession. Fifty prayers eventually became five, but it was that *Divine Light,* which Sayyidina Musa (Alayhi Salaam) wished to keep witnessing in the eyes of Sayyidina Rasulullah ﷺ (Salla lahu alayhi wa'ale hi Wasallam); the Light of the Witnessing of the Lord.

Upon returning to Makka, the Messenger ﷺ of Allah informed the people of this miraculous journey and heavenly ascent, but this led to the non-believers mocking this account, and trying to shake the faith of the believers. The pagans knew the journey from Makka to Jerusalem would take months, and beyond this with the Messenger ﷺ of Allah also saying that this miraculous journey was followed by the heavenly ascent, with all this taking place in one single night. This separated the believers, faithful men such as; Sayyidina Abu Bakr Siddique (RadiyAllahu Anhu), who was granted the title of 'truthful', from the ignorant doubters, cursed men like Abu Jahl, who's actual name was Abu'l Hakam, but received the title of *'Jahl'*, due to his ignorance. He asked Sayyidina Abu Bakr Siddique (Ra) of how he can believe such an account? Sayyidina Abu Bakr Siddique (RadiyAllahu Anhu) replied that, 'If Sayyidina Rasulullah ﷺ has said this then it is the truth. I declared belief that Allah (SWT) Is One, due to the *Shahadah* – Witnessing of the Messenger ﷺ of Allah'. The ones who refused to accept and mocked the Messenger ﷺ of Allah, were branded as ignorant, and lowered their places in the Hell fire. The ones who accepted that the most truthful can never lie, became known as the ones who support the truth. The trust and faith of the best of companions, the faith of Sayyidina Abu Bakr Siddique, May Allah (SWT) Be Pleased with him, would not be shaken upon being questioned by the disbelieving people of Makka.

The Messenger ﷺ of Allah, confirmed to the leaders of Makka that on the journey back from Jerusalem, there was a convoy who had lost their camel because it got scared from the sound of the Buraq, and they also had a vessel of water from which the Messenger ﷺ of Allah drank. The people of Makka said that they would wait for this convoy to arrive back to verify this. Allah (SWT) Supported the Messenger ﷺ of Allah, with great miracles, which included bringing Masjid Al Aqsa in front of the Messenger ﷺ of Allah, to describe its compound in detail. The Jewish people knew Al Aqsa very well. Allah (SWT) Held back the sun on this day, so that the convoy could safely arrive back to Makka and verify that they had seen the Messenger ﷺ of Allah. Had the sun set, they would not have returned back until the following day. It has been related that the sun has only been held back for the Messenger ﷺ of Allah, and for Sayyidina Yusha bin Nun (Alayhi Salaam) – *Joshua*. (Bayhaqi)

These miracles were not required for the believers, as the word of Sayyidina Rasulullah ﷺ (Salla lahu alayhi wa'ale hi Wasallam) is sufficient for them.

Hijrah

'If ye help him not, still Allah helped him when those who disbelieve drove him forth, the second of two; when they two were in the cave, when he said unto his comrade: Grieve not. Lo! Allah is with us'.

(Al Qur'an; 9:40)

The tribal chiefs of Makka plotted to assassinate the Messenger ﷺ of Allah, as they feared the spread of Islam. They knew that being from the tribe of Banu Hashim, this would lead to enmity with their tribe, so they selected one person from each of their tribes to carry out this terrible plan. This was the night when Allah (SWT) Had Ordered His Messenger ﷺ, to migrate to the town of Medina, and finally leave the city of Makka. This was a milestone in the establishment of Islam. Sayyidina Abu Bakr Siddique (RadiyAllahu Anhu) would be the one chosen to accompany the Messenger ﷺ of Allah. This was known as the *'Hijrah'*- the migration.

The enemies of Islam approached the house of Sayyidina Rasulullah ﷺ (Salla lahu alayhi wa'ale hi Wasallam), yet they were the same people who had entrusted their possessions with 'Al Ameen'. Such was the integrity, and honesty of Sayyidina Rasulullah ﷺ (Salla lahu alayhi wa'ale hi Wasallam) that even his ﷺ enemies trusted him the most.

Upon entering the house of the Messenger ﷺ of Allah, a miracle took place as the Messenger ﷺ of Allah walked past them, and even sprinkled dirt on their heads, yet they could not behold him ﷺ. Upon entering, they found the courageous and daring Sayyidina Ali ibn Abi Talib (Karamullah waj ho), May the Favour of Allah (SWT) Be upon him, occupying the blessed bed of the Messenger ﷺ of Allah. Sayyidina Ali ibn Abi Talib (RadiyAllahu Anhu) was the young cousin of the Messenger ﷺ of Allah, who had spent every day since childhood with him ﷺ. This is why one of the titles given to Sayyidina Ali ibn Abi

Talib (Ra), is *'Baab-e-Rasul'* – Gateway to the Messenger ﷺ. This is based on the authentic narration of the Messenger ﷺ of Allah, *'I am the city of knowledge, Ali is the gate'*. (Tirmidhi). This implies the closeness of Sayyidina Ali ibn Abi Talib (Ra), with the Messenger ﷺ of Allah, and the fact that Sayyidina Ali ibn Abi Talib (Ra) observed the Messenger ﷺ closely from a young age, and took knowledge from him ﷺ. Sayyidina Ali ibn Abi Talib (Ra) is the lion of Islam, the one who risked his life, by putting himself in place of the Messenger ﷺ of Allah that night as the attackers approached.

On this night of the *'Hijrah'*, the migration took place as Sayyidina Rasulullah ﷺ (Salla lahu alayhi wa'ale hi Wasallam) departed from Makka t'ul Makkaramah to Medina t'ul Munnawarah. Sayyidina Abu Bakr Siddique (RadiyAllahu Anhu) is mentioned in the Noble Qur'an, as the *'companion of the cave'*. This verse referred to the cave of *'Thaur'*. The Messenger ﷺ of Allah, along with Sayyidina Abu Bakr Siddique (Ra), stayed in this cave, as the pagans of Makka pursued them. The Messenger ﷺ rested his ﷺ blessed head in the lap of Sayyidina Abu Bakr Siddique (Ra) and went to sleep. Sayyidina Abu Bakr Siddique (Ra), whose duty was to safeguard the Messenger ﷺ of Allah, noticed that a gap in the wall had not been checked for dangerous creatures. Sayyidina Abu Bakr Siddique (Ra) raised his leg and placed his foot in this hole to block it. He kept his foot inside this hole while the Messenger ﷺ of Allah slept. There was a scorpion in that hole, and it bit the foot of Sayyidina Abu Bakr Siddique (Ra) repeatedly. Sayyidina Abu Bakr Siddique (RadiyAllahu Anhu) did not move, and endured the pain, in his love for the Messenger ﷺ of Allah, as he did not wish to wake the Messenger ﷺ of Allah.

Sayyidina Rasulullah ﷺ (Salla lahu alayhi wa'ale hi Wasallam) and his ﷺ faithful companion (RadiyAllahu Anhu) reached the city of Medina, which lit up with *Nur* – Light. Authentic traditions confirm that this was actual light that illuminated the city of Medina when the Messenger ﷺ of Allah entered. The city was since re-named Medina t'ul Munawwarah, meaning the *'City of illumination'*. The residents of Medina celebrated the arrival of the Messenger ﷺ of Allah, and all the people of Medina wished for the Messenger ﷺ of Allah to be their guest. The Messenger ﷺ of Allah decided that wherever his ﷺ camel would stop, this place would host the Messenger ﷺ of Allah. The blessed camel of Sayyidina Rasulullah ﷺ (Salla lahu alayhi wa'ale hi Wasallam) walked through the city and first stopped at a place, lowering his head. The camel then continued until reaching the house of Sayyidina Abu Ayub Ansari (RadiyAllahu Anhu). His actual name was 'Khalid'. This is where the Messenger ﷺ of Allah stayed until his ﷺ own blessed house was built. The first place where the camel had lowered its head, was the site of *'Masjid-e-Nabi'*, which is the Mosque of the Prophet ﷺ. This is where the first Masjid in Medina t'ul Munnawwarah was later built. The believers of Medina t'ul Munnawwarah, were known as the *'Ansaaar'*. This means *'the helpers'*, as they welcomed the believers of Makka with open arms, sharing everything they had with their companions. The blessings of the people of the *'Ansaar'* can still be seen today in the warmth and love of the residents of Medina.

Badr

The first battle in Islam was the battle of *'Badr'*. Allah (SWT) Ordered His Final Messenger ﷺ (Salla lahu alayhi wa'ale hi Wasallam) to enter the battlefield with the faithful companions (RadiyAllahu Anhumma) to defend Islam and oppose falsehood and tyranny. The struggle was always for Islam whether it was in the form of endurance and forbearance, in the face of severe persecution, or by displaying courage and the height of faith, when faced with insurmountable opposition, against large armies on the battlefield.

The Messenger ﷺ of Allah, has only ever acted upon Divine Revelation and Inspiration, and this enabled his ﷺ faithful companions, May Allah (SWT) Be Pleased with them, to follow the straight path, through following the way of the Messenger ﷺ of Allah. This is referred to as the *'Sunnah'*, the 'Path' of the Messenger ﷺ of Allah. The State of Medina had been established as the first Muslim State. This was opposed by the powerful leaders of the Quraysh, and they marched to confront this State. They were met by the believers, who were not equipped to face an army three times their size, but they were led by the Leader of all Creation; the Final Messenger; Sayyidina Rasulullah ﷺ (Salla lahu alayhi wa'ale hi Wasallam). Allah (SWT) Sent tranquillity into their hearts, so that they stood in 'Badr' on the threshold of the first Islamic victory. The day of 'Badr', the believers were three hundred and thirteen in number and their enemies had the numbers on their side as they outnumbered the believers by three times. Allah (SWT) Cleansed the warriors with the truth and gave them victory over the enemies of Islam. The believers lived by the faith of the Divine Word of Allah (SWT) and the blessed touch of the Messenger ﷺ of Allah. On the plains of Badr, the Muslims who were mainly farmers, and carpenters, with little weaponry, fought for every Word revealed in the Glorious Qur'an, and bled for their unquenchable love for the Final

Messenger ﷺ. The believers fought their own kin as family members of the companions (Ra) who they had left behind, were fighting as their enemies, but the resolve of the believers was unshakeable. The angels descended in Badr, to fight alongside the Muslims, and give them victory against a greater number, who had the best of means, yet could not defeat the men who stood like mountains. SubhanAllah.

Uhud

Victory in Badr, showed the faith of the believers, and that they would overcome the enemy through the truth Bestowed upon them. The Messenger ﷺ of Allah, showed his ﷺ humanity, by treating the prisoners of War as guests, instructing the Companions (RadiyAllahu Anhumma) to bring the best food they have for them. As ransom, the Messenger ﷺ of Allah, requested the learned people among the captives to teach the believers how to read and write. The Messenger ﷺ of Allah, brought a religion of humanity, which united people of all divisions, whether that was of colour, caste or creed. Anyone who experienced the mercy of the Messenger ﷺ of Allah, was drawn to this faith. As the captives from the battle of Badr returned to Makka, they spoke of the hospitality of the Muslims of Medina, and the humanity of their religion.

The enemies of Islam came again after suffering defeat at the hands of the Muslimeen in Badr. This time on a mountain called Uhud, the enemies of Islam gathered an even greater army in the hope to defeat the message of Sayyidina Rasulullah ﷺ (Salla lahu alayhi wa'ale hi Wasallam). In the land of Badr, the courage of the believers was displayed and now on the Mount of Uhud, it was time for the patience of the Muslims to be tested. The believers had tasted victory as the enemy fled, only to be ambushed from behind as a group of Muslim soldiers failed to guard the mountain as ordered by the Messenger ﷺ of Allah. This was a sign given to the believers of the consequence of failing to obey even a single word uttered by the Messenger ﷺ of Allah.

On Uhud, the brave Uncle of the Messenger ﷺ of Allah; Sayyidina Hamza Ibn Abdul Muttalib (RadiyAllahu Anhu), who was only one of two Uncles of the Messenger ﷺ who openly accepted Islam, was martyred. The Messenger ﷺ of Allah was also injured. Sayyidina Rasulullah ﷺ (Salla lahu alayhi wa'ale hi Wasallam) grieved for his ﷺ

beloved Uncle, and the lovers of the blessed Messenger ﷺ of Allah, grieved upon hearing of the injuries suffered by him ﷺ.

Sayyidina Owais Qarni (RadiyAllahu Anhu) was a dervish, who was from a place called, 'Qarn'. Upon hearing, and according to some reports witnessing through spiritual enlightenment, the blessed face of the Messenger ﷺ of Allah being injured, and losing a blessed tooth in Uhud, Sayyidina Owais Qarni (RadiyAllahu Anhu) smashed his own teeth using a rock, to remove the same tooth that Sayyidina Rasulullah ﷺ (Salla lahu alayhi wa'ale hi Wasallam) had lost. Sayyidina Owais Qarni (Ra) did not actually get a chance to meet the Messenger ﷺ of Allah in person, yet was honoured with being a companion out of his extreme love for the Messenger ﷺ of Allah.

The great martyrs were laid to rest at Uhud, this was the Mount which trembled under the weight of Sayyidina Rasulullah ﷺ (Salla lahu alayhi wa'ale hi Wasallam), the great martyr Sayyidina Hamza ibn Abdul Muttalib (RadiyAllahu Anhu); and the great Siddique; Sayyidina Abu Bakr Siddique (RadiyAllahu Anhu). The Messenger ﷺ of Allah is reported to have said about Uhud, as recorded in authentic hadith; *"This is a mountain which loves us and is loved by us."* (Sahih Bukhari)

The Growth of Islam

Islam spread all over Arabia, through the growing legacy of Sayyidina Rasulullah ﷺ (Salla lahu alayhi wa'ale hi Wasallam). Idol worshipping, soothsayers and atheism were abandoned, in favour of worshipping Allah (SWT) the Only One worthy of worship. Islam spread equality through the land, maintaining the ties of kinship and demonstrating the highest morals and manners. Islam abolished slavery and oppression towards women, as even the hardest opponents of Islam submitted to the Will of Allah (SWT), adopting the beautiful conduct of Sayyidina Rasulullah ﷺ (Salla lahu alayhi wa'ale hi Wasallam). The hardest of hearts melted as they accepted the true faith. Islam taught that education is for all regardless of caste and colour and the slaves became scholars of the age, becoming dignified men who were given status through their belief in Islam. Women no longer feared for their life, as they were given security and equality through the rulings of the Islamic Shariah.

The Messenger of Allah ﷺ led the way and displayed the highest ideals of conduct for all to see and learn from. In the age when idolaters buried their daughters alive, Sayyidina Rasulullah ﷺ (Salla lahu alayhi wa'ale hi Wasallam) honoured his ﷺ blessed wives and daughters. Allah SWT) Had taken away his ﷺ blessed sons in infancy, and the fact that the best ﷺ of all creation had four daughters, showed all of society the blessing of raising daughters.

When Christians saw the Muslims in *Shaam* - Syria, they accepted that the followers of Sayyidina Eesa (Alayhi Salaam) - *Jesus Christ*, are not better than the followers of Sayyidina Muhammad ﷺ (Salla lahu alayhi wa'ale hi Wasallam). In fact, even the miracles revealed upon Sayyidina Eesa (As), Peace be upon him, did not match those seen in the apparent life of Sayyidina Rasulullah ﷺ (Salla lahu alayhi wa'ale hi Wasallam). Sayyidina Eesa - Jesus (As) according to traditions, brought no more than fifteen miracles in their apparent life, yet Sayyidina Rasulullah ﷺ (Salla lahu alayhi wa'ale hi Wasallam) had thousands of miracles reported in authentic accounts. Through the Will of Allah (SWT), Sayyidina Eesa – *Jesus*, Peace be upon him, had the miracle of bringing the dead to life, returning the attribute of life to the one who had it no longer, yet Sayyidina Rasulullah ﷺ (Salla lahu alayhi wa'ale hi Wasallam) brought attributes of life, speech and feelings to things that were not created with them. Sayyidina Rasulullah ﷺ (Salla lahu alayhi wa'ale hi Wasallam); the Final Messenger, summoned a tree and the tree walked as ordered by him ﷺ. (Sahih Bukhari). Animals were able to converse with the Messenger ﷺ of Allah, on many occasions, and the pebbles of Abu Jahl recited the Kalima.

An incident reported in books of ahadith, mention that the Messenger ﷺ of Allah would deliver sermons in the early days in Medina t'ul Munuwwarah, while leaning against a trunk of a date palm tree. Later, a pulpit was built for the Messenger ﷺ of Allah, and on the day when the Messenger ﷺ of Allah left the date tree, and walked over to the newly built pulpit, the tree trunk was heard weeping. This crying out of separation from the Messenger ﷺ of Allah, was heard by all those assembled in the Masjid. Sayyidina Rasulullah ﷺ (Salla lahu alayhi wa'ale hi Wasallam walked over to the date palm tree, and placed his ﷺ blessed hand on it, to stop it from weeping. (Sahih Bukhari). The blessed touch of Sayyidina Rasulullah ﷺ (Salla lahu alayhi wa'ale hi wasallam) brought peace and security to this old tree, and showed that the entire creation longs for the Messenger ﷺ of Allah.

Sayyidina Musa (Alayhi Salaam) - *Moses*, Peace be upon him, would use his staff to derive water from a rock, and another Prophet of Allah; Sayyidina Isma'il (As), the forefather of the Messenger ﷺ of Allah, as a baby rubbed his blessed feet on the barren ground to produce the water of Zamzam. Water can be found in these places, and the blessed Prophets of Allah, May Allah Bless them with Eternal Peace, produced miracles when required. Yet water came out of the fingers of the Final Messenger ﷺ (Salla lahu alayhi wa'ale hi Wasallam), which was sufficient for one thousand companions who performed ablution with this miracle. (Sahih Bukhari). This miracle is even greater than those attributed to the preceding Prophets, Peace be upon them, as water does not exist in our fingers, yet Allah (SWT) attributed this to His most blessed Messenger ﷺ. The Books of Seerah, have recorded thousands of such miracles.

Hudaybiyah

'Those who pledge allegiance to you, actually pledge allegiance to Allah'.

(Al Qur'an; 48:10)

The Messenger ﷺ of Allah was ordered to begin performing the pilgrimage to the House of Allah (SWT) in Makka. The Messenger ﷺ of Allah, made the journey along with his ﷺ Companions (RadiyAllahu Anhumma), and their convoy stopped at a place outside of Makka, which is called 'Hudaybiyah'. The Messenger ﷺ of Allah, wished to know whether the Leaders of Makka would accept their entry, so instructed one of his ﷺ faithful companions; Sayyidina Uthman ibn Affan (RadiyAllahu Anhu) to enter Makka and negotiate terms with the leaders of Quraysh.

Sayyidina Uthman ibn Affan (RadiyAllahu Anhu) who had been one of the first to migrate with his family in the cause of Islam, entered Makka and met with the chiefs of Quraysh, informing them that they had not come to fight, but to visit the *Baitullah Sharif*; the Holy Kaaba, universally recognized as the House of Allah (SWT). Sayyidina Uthman Ibn Affan (Ra) met Aban bin Sa`id bin Al-`As upon entering Makkah, and Aban took Sayyidina Uthman (Ra) with him and extended his protection to him so he could deliver his message to Abu Sufyan. When Sayyidina Uthman Ibn Affan (Ra) spoke with Abu Sufyan, who had led two armies against the believers in Badr and Uhud, he agreed that his own associate will go to negotiate directly with the Messenger ﷺ of Allah, but extended hospitality to Sayyidina Uthman Ibn Affan (Ra), with an offer that as he is already in Makka, he can go ahead and perform Umrah – *minor pilgrimage*. Sayyidina Uthman Ibn Affan (RadiyAllahu Anhu) replied, `I would not do that without the Messenger ﷺ of Allah'. So the Quraysh kept Sayyidina Uthman (RadiyAllahu Anhu) in Makkah, while a representative of Abu Sufyan would go to Hudaybiyah.

In Hudaybiyah, the Muslims heard rumours that Sayyidina Uthman Ibn Affan (Ra) had been killed. Sayyidina Rasulullah ﷺ (Salla lahu alayhi wa'ale hi Wasallam) told the companions that 'We will not leave until we fight these people for the killing of Uthman'. Sayyidina Rasulullah ﷺ (Salla lahu alayhi wa'ale hi Wasallam) called the Muslims at Hudaybiyah to give a pledge of allegiance, which was later known as the pledge of *'Ar-Ridwan'*. This pledge was given on the hand of the Messenger ﷺ of Allah to fight with honour till death, and this pledge took place under a tree. The verse was revealed in the Noble Quran, about this pledge;

'Those who pledge allegiance to you, actually pledge allegiance to Allah. The Hand of Allah is above their hands. So whosoever breaks his oath, breaks it only to his soul's hurt; while whosoever keep his Covenant with Allah, on him will He bestow immense reward.'.

(Al Qur'an; 48:10)

Allah (SWT) Revealing to the believers that the pledge given by them to His Final Messenger ﷺ, is in reality a Pledge to Allah (SWT), and includes His Acceptance. This is the honour bestowed upon Sayyidina Rasulullah ﷺ (Salla lahu alayhi wa'ale hi Wasallam). The *'Pledge of Ar-Ridwan'*, is also one of the signs of the honour of Sayyidina Uthman Ibn Affan (RadiyAllahu Anhu), as the Messenger ﷺ of Allah placed his ﷺ own blessed hand over the other hand, and said, *'This is on behalf of Uthman'*. (Sahih Bukhari). The Messenger ﷺ of Allah pledging allegiance on behalf of Sayyidina Uthman Ibn Affan (RadiyAllahu Anhu) gave him a unique honour of having the blessed hand of the Messenger ﷺ of Allah represent his own hand in this pledge. Also, Sayyidina Uthman Ibn Affan (Ra) received two of the blessed daughters of the Messenger ﷺ of Allah in marriage. Sayyidina Ruqaiyya (RadiyAllahu Anha) was married to Sayyidina Uthman Ibn

Affan (RadiyAllahu Anhu) and after her passing away, Allah (SWT) Commanded that the younger sister; Sayyidina Ummi Kulthum (RadiyAllahu Anha) be given in marriage to Sayyidina Uthman Ibn Affan (RadiyAllahu Anhu). This honour earned Sayyidina Uthman Ibn Affan (Ra) the title of; *'Dhū al-Nurayn'* ("The Possessor of **Two** Lights"). (Ash'aam-il).

When Allah (SWT) mentions the *'Pledge of Ar-Ridwan'*, (Al Qur'an 48:10), He states *'The Hand of Allah is above their hands'*. The meaning of this verse is that those who gave their hands in the blessed hand of the Messenger ﷺ of Allah, have Allah's (SWT) Favour and Acceptance.

'But no, by your Lord, they can have no real faith until they make you judge in all disputes between them, and find in their-selves no resistance against your decisions, and submit with the fullest submission'. **(Al Qur'an; 4:65)**

This above verse was proof to the Companions (RadiyAllahu Anhumma) that they must accept every judgement from the Messenger ﷺ of Allah, as being the Divine Order of Allah (SWT). This was tested when the delegates of the Quraysh came to negotiate with the Messenger ﷺ of Allah. The terms they put forward were not favourable to the believers but Sayyidina Rasulullah ﷺ (Salla lahu alayhi wa'ale hi Wasallam) accepted them in exchange for access to the blessed city of Makka. The terms would allow the believers to perform the pilgrimage beginning from the following year, but all terms in the agreement favoured the Quraysh. As part of the agreement, the delegates from Makka would not even allow the Messenger ﷺ of Allah, to include his ﷺ blessed title of *'Rasulullah'* – 'Messenger ﷺ of Allah', on the agreement, and had to sign as Muhammad ﷺ ibn Abdullah. This particularly angered the believers, especially Sayyidina Umar Ibn Khattab (Ra) who was known for his passion and vigour.

The Companions (RadiyAllahu Anhumma) felt that the terms of the treaty of Hudaybiyah were insulting to them and moreso because of the fact that they were not allowed to enter Makka that year. The terms of the treaty stated they can perform Umrah the following year. Here once again the virtues of Sayyidina Abu Bakr Siddique (RadiyAllahu Anhu) were made apparent. Sayyidina Abu Bakr Siddique (Ra) had such a close and deep relationship with Sayyidina Rasulullah ﷺ (Salla lahu alayhi wa'ale hi Wasallam) that on many issues, Sayyidina Abu Bakr Siddique (Ra) would hold the same opinion as that of the Messenger ﷺ of Allah. At Hudaybiyah, the believers felt humiliated by the terms agreed and many among the younger companions could not bear it. Sayyidina Umar Ibn Khattab (Ra) anxiously came to Sayyidina Rasulullah ﷺ (Salla lahu alayhi wa'ale hi Wasallam) and asked, 'O Messenger ﷺ of Allah, are you not the truthful Prophet of Allah?' Sayyidina Rasulullah ﷺ (Salla lahu alayhi wa'ale hi Wasallam) replied: 'Indeed, I am'. Sayyidina Umar Ibn Khattab (Ra) then asked, 'Are we not on The Haq (True Path) and the enemy on falsehood?' The Messenger ﷺ of Allah replied: 'Truly indeed'. Sayyidina Umar Ibn Khattab (Ra) then asked, 'Then why are we being degraded in this manner?' Sayyidina Rasulullah ﷺ (Salla lahu alayhi wa'ale hi Wasallam) replied: 'I am the Messenger ﷺ of Allah, and I cannot disobey Him. Verily He is my Protector'. Sayyidina Umar Ibn Khattab (RadiyAllahu Anhu), then asked, 'Did you not say to us that we are going to Makkah, and are going to perform Umrah?' Sayyidina Rasulullah ﷺ (Salla lahu alayhi wa'ale hi Wasallam) smiled, 'Verily it is true, but did I say that we will perform it this year?' Sayyidina 'Umar Ibn Khattab (Ra) replied: 'No, you did not say this'. Sayyidina Rasulullah ﷺ, said: 'We will surely go to Makka and perform Umrah'. Sayyidina Umar Ibn Khattab (Ra) discussed this with Sayyidina Abu Bakr Siddique (RadiyAllahu Anhu), asking him, 'O Abu Bakr, is this not the truthful Prophet of Allah?' Sayyidina Abu Bakr Siddique (Ra) replied: 'Verily, yes'. Sayyidina Umar Ibn Khattab (Ra) then asked: 'Are we not on the truth and the non-believers on falsehood?' Sayyidina Abu Bakr Siddique (Ra) replied in the affirmative. Sayyidina Umar Ibn Khattab (Ra) then asked: 'Why are we being disgraced in this manner for our deen?' Sayyidina Abu Bakr Siddique (RadiyAllahu Anhu) replied: 'O man, without doubt, the Messenger ﷺ is the truthful Prophet of Allah, and does not disobey Allah (SWT) in the least, and Allah

(SWT) is his ﷺ Protector. Hold fast unto his ﷺ reigns'. Sayyidina Umar Ibn Khattab (Ra) then asked, 'Did the Messenger ﷺ of Allah not say that we will be going to Makka, and will be performing the Umrah?' Sayyidina Abu Bakr Siddique (Ra) replied: 'Did the Messenger ﷺ promise you that we will go this year?' Sayyidina Umar Ibn Khattab (Ra) replied: 'No, the Messenger ﷺ of Allah did not say this to us'. Sayyidina Abu Bakr Siddique (Ra), replied, 'Insha'Allah, you will go to Makkah and will also perform Umrah '. The responses of Sayyidina Abu Bakr Siddique (RadiyAllahu Anhu) reflected those of the Messenger ﷺ of Allah. In Sufi traditions, a true student is one who emulates his teacher in every regard, even in their mannerisms and habits.

Sayyidina Abu Bakr Siddique (RadiyAllahu Anhu) was honoured as being the best after the Prophets of Allah (SWT), Peace be upon them all. Sayyidina Abu Bakr Siddique (Ra) has been mentioned in the 'Noble Qur'an', described as the *'companion of the cave'* (Al Qur'an 9:40). During the Hijrah, the migration to Medina, the Messenger ﷺ of Allah, was accompanied only by Sayyidina Abu Bakr Siddique (Ra), and when during their refuge in a cave, as the enemies approached, the verse was revealed to the Messenger ﷺ of Allah, when Sayyidina Abu Bakr Siddique (Ra) enquired whether the enemies would see them,

'Do not grieve; Indeed Allah is with us'. (Al Qur'an; 9:40).

These are three great virtues of Sayyidina Abu Bakr Siddique (RadiyAllahu Anhu). The first, to have unity and a close relationship with Sayyidina Rasulullah ﷺ (Salla lahu alayhi wa'ale hi Wasallam), and to have assisted him ﷺ during the migration. The second as being addressed by Allah (SWT), as the *'companion'* of the Messenger ﷺ of Allah, as revealed in 'Surah 9, verse 40', and thirdly this revelation of being in the company of Allah (SWT) and the Messenger ﷺ of Allah. This is the meaning of the verse revealed to the Messenger ﷺ of Allah for his ﷺ faithful companion; *'Allah is with us'*. At this time only Sayyidina Rasulullah ﷺ (Salla lahu alayhi wa'ale hi Wasallam) and Sayyidina Abu Bakr Siddique (RadiyAllahu Anhu) were present.

The events of 'Hudaybiyah' were evidence as were the events of Uhud that complete submission to the orders and decisions of Sayyidina Rasulullah ﷺ (Salla lahu alayhi wa'ale hi Wasallam) is the true meaning of Submission to Allah (SWT). The companions (RadiyAllahu Anhumma) accepted that the Messenger ﷺ of Allah only acts from inspiration from Allah (SWT), as stated in the Noble Qur'an;

'And he does not speak from his own choice, no, it is but revelation divinely revealed'.

(Al Qur'an; 53:3-4)

Allah (SWT) showed His tremendous favour on His beloved Messenger ﷺ in the verses mentioned. Allah (SWT) Made the judgement of His Final Messenger ﷺ as His own Judgement in all matters, his ﷺ order as His own decree in all affairs. Allah (SWT) does not accept the faith of the believers in His Divinity, until they have accepted and submitted to the commands of Sayyidina Rasulullah ﷺ (Salla lahu alayhi wa'ale hi Wasallam),

Urwa bin Masud came as the ambassador of the leaders of Quraysh, to negotiate with the Messenger ﷺ of Allah at Hudaybiyah. He returned and described the love the Companions (RadiyAllahu Anhumma) had for the Messenger ﷺ of Allah. It has been narrated that he told the people of Makka upon his return that he had watched the Companions (Ra) closely, he noticed that they did not even let the blessed saliva of the Messenger ﷺ of Allah touch the ground, rather they caught it in their hands one after the other, and rubbed it on their faces and over their body. He narrated that the order of the Messenger ﷺ of Allah was obeyed at once, and when the Messenger ﷺ of Allah performed ablution, his ﷺ companions would rush and collect the water that touched his ﷺ blessed body, and would excel in this with each other. They would keep their eyes lowered in his ﷺ presence, out of reverence for the Messenger ﷺ, and would keep their tone lowered when addressing him ﷺ. Urwa bin Masud, said, 'O People, by the Lord, I have been to the courts of Kings, with delegations, I have attended the court of Chosroes, Caesar, and Negus, but I have never seen a King who has followers with the respect like the companions have for the Messenger ﷺ of Allah. By God, they collect his ﷺ blessed saliva in their hands, and rub it over their hands and body, they collect his ﷺ used water of ablution, and would be ready to fight for it. They keep their voices lowered in his ﷺ presence, and never gaze at him ﷺ out of respect'. (Sahih Bukhari)

Al Fath – The Victory

'We have given you a clear victory ….' (Al Qur'an; 48:1)

Allah (SWT) Perfected His favour and blessings upon Sayyidina Rasulullah ﷺ (Salla lahu alayhi wa'ale hi Wasallam), confirming his ﷺ law - shariah will prevail and the above verses continue with Allah (SWT) Revealing; *'forgiven him for past and present'*.

The 'Forgiveness' of Allah (SWT) here is His Favour and Bounties upon the Messenger ﷺ of Allah, as the Messenger ﷺ is free from sin. The term 'forgiveness' in this context is a 'Mercy' upon the Messenger ﷺ of Allah, and is further explained in the next verses that Allah (SWT) Has *'completed His blessing'* upon him ﷺ. This meaning the conquest of Makka and Taif.   (Kitab'Ash-Shifa)

The treaty of Hudaybiyah opened the doors to Makka, allowing believers to visit and spread the message of Islam. Eventually the people of Quraysh had submitted, even the most powerful opponent of all; Abu Sufyan accepted Islam. The believers marched onto Makka t'ul Makkaramah, with victory already granted and no resistance shown as the blessed city was taken by the believers. Sayyidina Rasulullah ﷺ (Salla lahu alayhi wa'ale hi Wasallam) entered in complete humility, and Submission to Allah (SWT). The blessed eyes of the Messenger ﷺ of Allah, lowered even in this moment of ultimate triumph, over people who had tortured and mocked him ﷺ and his ﷺ blessed companions (Ra).

When the Messenger ﷺ of Allah entered Makka as a conqueror, its inhabitants became frightened. There was no place to live nor a path to walk. Sayyidina Rasulullah ﷺ (Salla lahu alayhi wa'ale hi Wasallam) was well known for being merciful and generous, and upon entering announced that the person who entered the House of Allah - *Kaaba* was safe, and those who remained in their homes were also safe. The ones who laid down their arms were also guaranteed security.

However, there were eleven men and six women whose crimes could not be forgiven. These people were not included in the general amnesty. It was announced that there was no mercy for these people. Among them, seven of the men and two women embraced Islam, and were subsequently pardoned. The remaining four men and four women were killed. Ibn Khatl was one of the eight that were punished. He had accepted Islam initially but later became an apostate and went to Makka. He then began to dis-respect the Messenger ﷺ of Allah through shameful poetry. For this reason, despite him entering the Harem of the Kaaba, he was also killed. This was an exception to the Universal Law of Allah (SWT), which is that blood is not shed in the *'Harem'* of the Kaaba. This is the blessed sanctuary where since the time of Sayyidina Ibrahim (Alayhi Salaam), anyone who enters would not be harmed, as fighting and killing is forbidden within this Sanctuary. Yet Allah (SWT) Revealed to the Messenger ﷺ of Allah that Ibn Khatl had committed the sin of transgressing the honour of the Messenger ﷺ of Allah, and he would not be protected by the Sanctuary of the Kaaba. A person came and said, "O' Messenger ﷺ of Allah, Ibn Khatl is clinging to the cloth of the Kaaba." Sayyidina Rasulullah ﷺ (Salla lahu alayhi wa'ale hi Wasallam) replied, "He is not of the ones who have been granted amnesty, kill him." Ibn Shihaab Zuhri says, "I have been informed that the Messenger ﷺ of Allah was not in the state of *Ihraam.*"
The Messenger ﷺ of Allah has said, *"This was permissible for me today (not wearing Ihraam) and not for any other person."* (Ash'Shaam'il Muhammidiyah ﷺ)

The Shariah has made it obligatory for any person entering Makka, to be in a state of 'Ihraam', which is being clad in two unstitched white garments. They must perform the Umrah, the minor pilgrimage, before leaving the state of Ihraam. However, the Messenger ﷺ of Allah entered, not in a state of Ihraam, and this was only permissible for him ﷺ

The events of the conquest of Makka clearly show the elevated rank of Sayyidina Rasulullah ﷺ (Salla lahu alayhi wa'ale hi Wasallam) providing evidence any person who commits the sin of slandering the Messenger ﷺ of Allah, was not even pardoned despite being in the sanctuary of the 'Harem'. Allah (SWT) is the Sole guide of Sayyidina Rasulullah ﷺ (Salla lahu alayhi wa'ale hi Wasallam) and the fact the beloved Messenger ﷺ of Allah, gave such an order confirms that there is none more dear or sacred to Allah (SWT) than His Final Messenger ﷺ. Also, the Messenger ﷺ of Allah entered Makka to conquer, without being in a State of Ihraam. The authentic narrations confirm that the Messenger ﷺ of Allah, said *'Only Makka is halaal for me today'*. (Tirmidhi)

The great companion, the former Abyssinian Slave, Sayyidina Bilal ibn Rabah (RadiyAllahu Anhu) was instructed to climb on top of the Kaaba, and give the *Adhaan* – Call to Prayer. This very act of elevating a slave who had been liberated by Islam, the man who had been severely tortured by his owner, after accepting Islam, before being freed by Sayyidina Abu Bakr Siddique (RadiyAllahu Anhu), showed the equality within this faith. As the believers took Makka, the Messenger ﷺ of Allah elevated the status of the ones who were considered inferior by their society, above the heights of what was considered sacred by the same people who had oppressed them.

The people of Makka were brought in front of the Messenger ﷺ of Allah, who asked them, "O Quraysh, what do you expect from me today?" They replied, "Mercy, O Prophet of Allah. We expect nothing but good from you." The Messenger ﷺ of Allah declared:" Today I will speak to you as Yusuf spoke to his brothers. I will not harm you and Allah will forgive you for He is Merciful and Loving. Go you are free." (Ibn Kathir). Sayyidina Rasulullah ﷺ (Salla lahu alayhi wa'ale hi Wasallam) forgave the killing of his ﷺ beloved Uncle; Sayyidina Hamza Ibn Abdul Muttalib (RadiyAllahu Anhu); and his ﷺ faithful companions such as; Sayyidina Sumayya bint Khabbat (RadiyAllahu Anha), who was among the great female companions, and the first martyr in Islam. Also forgave the persecution of the believers, and the fact that the Messenger ﷺ of Allah had himself suffered unlimited torment at their hands, and was forced to leave his ﷺ city of Makka. The Messenger ﷺ of Allah, cited the words of another Prophet of Allah; Sayyidina Yusuf (Alayhi Salaam) - *Joseph*, who forgave his brothers who had tried to kill him, after having authority over them. All was forgiven, as his ﷺ most powerful enemies embraced Islam and gave the city over to him ﷺ. As the Messenger ﷺ of Allah entered the Kaaba, where the idols were kept, they fell in submission to his ﷺ testimony of 'La illaha illa'Allah; Muhammad'ur ﷺ Rasulullah'.

Separation from the Messenger ﷺ of Allah

Sayyidina Rasulullah ﷺ (Salla lahu alayhi wa'ale hi Wasallam) later performed the obligatory pilgrimage – Hajj, and this pilgrimage was known as the 'Farewell Pilgrimage'. On the day of Arafat, the Messenger ﷺ of Allah delivered the 'Farewell Sermon' – *Khutba t'ul Wada*. This sermon addressed the believers, warning them against the deception of *Shaytaan* – the devil, and against competing for worldly gains. The Messenger ﷺ of Allah informed them that a person cannot be superior to another as a result of their heritage; colour; caste; or creed, but only through their piety. The Messenger ﷺ of Allah reminded his ﷺ community that they must fulfil their rights towards each other, including what has been entrusted to them, and fulfil the rights of their women, and treat them with kindness. The Messenger ﷺ advised all believers to remain steadfast in worshipping Allah (SWT); by praying their five times salaah; fasting in Ramadan; paying Zakaat – *charity;* and performing Hajj, if having the means to do so.

Finally, Sayyidina Rasulullah ﷺ (Salla lahu alayhi wa'ale hi Wasallam) said as narrated by Sayyidina Abdullah Ibn Mas'ud (Ra),

'O People, no prophet or apostle will come after me and no new faith will be born. Reason well, therefore, O People, and understand words which I convey to you. I leave behind two things, the Book and my Sunnah, and if you follow these you will never go astray.

All those who listen to me shall pass on my words to others and those to others again; and may the last ones understand my words better than those who listen to me directly. Be my witness, O Allah, that I have conveyed your message to your people".

(Sahih Bukhari)

In the gathering at Arafat, some of the Sahaabah (RadiyAllahu Anhumma) began to weep as they listened to these final words. They understood that the time had come when the Messenger ﷺ of Allah would depart.

Shortly after performing the Farewell Hajj - *Pilgrimage*, Messenger ﷺ of Allah departed from this temporary abode.

It has been narrated by the Companions, May Allah (SWT) Be Pleased with them, when the Messenger ﷺ of Allah entered Medina, everything became illuminated. (Tirmidhi). This was actual light that became present in Medina, and this is why this city became known as the illuminated city; Medina t'ul Munnawwarah. It has been narrated from the blessed Companions (RadiyAllahu Anhumma);

'When the anwaar - illumination increased, it could be felt. In the dark nights of Ramadan many a time because of the intensity of the anwaaraat (illuminations), a natural illumination, was felt. But the day when Sayyidina Rasulullah ﷺ (Salla lahu alayhi wa'ale hi Wasallam) passed away, everything in Medina became darker. This light faded from the city.

We had not yet dusted off the dust from our hands after the burial of Sayyidina Rasulullah ﷺ (Salla lahu alayhi wa'ale hi Wasallam), when we began to feel the change in our hearts.'

(Ash'Shaam-il Muhammidiyyah ﷺ)

This does not mean that a change took place in their level of belief or love to perform good deeds, but they missed the bounties of the noble company of the Messenger ﷺ of Allah, and being in his ﷺ illuminated presence. The illumination of his ﷺ presence among them could not be benefited from anymore. Also, the Divine Revelations ceased with the departure of Sayyidina Rasulullah ﷺ (Salla lahu alayhi wa'ale hi Wasallam). The Messenger ﷺ of Allah is the *'Seal'*, the Finality of Prophethood and Messengership. Many of the Sahaabah (RadiyAllahu Anhumma) did not believe that Sayyidina Rasulullah ﷺ (Salla lahu alayhi wa'ale hi Wasallam) would ever depart. However it was Sayyidina Abu Bakr Siddique (Ra) who had begun leading the prayer in the final days of the apparent stay in this world of the Messenger ﷺ of Allah, this was due to his ﷺ illness. Sayyidina Abu Bakr Siddique (RadiyAllahu Anhu) reminded the believers that the Messenger ﷺ of Allah was to depart as the Messengers, Peace be upon them all, before him ﷺ had departed.

Sayyidina Aayeshaa Siddiqua (RadiyAllahu Anha) says that: "After the passing of Sayyidina Rasulullah ﷺ (Salla lahu alayhi wa'ale hi Wasallam), Sayyidina Abu Bakr Siddique (RadiyAllahu Anhu) entered, kissed him ﷺ on his ﷺ blessed lower forehead (between the eyes), and put his hands on the blessed shoulders of Sayyidina Rasulullah ﷺ (Salla lahu alayhi wa'ale hi Wasallam) and said: 'Waa Nabiyyaah, Waa Safiyyaah, Waa Khalilaah".

(Ash-Shama'il Muhammidiyah ﷺ)

Ever-lasting Legacy

'Did We not Exalt you in your fame'.

(Al Qur'an 94:4)

The subsequent era began of the *'Khulafa-e-Rashideen'*, the Rightly Guided Caliphs. Beginning with the best of the Sahaabah (RadiyAllahu Anhumma); Sayyidina Abu Bakr Siddique; then being succeeded by Sayyidina Umar ibn Khattab; followed by Sayyidina Uthman Ibn Affan; then on to Sayyidina Ali ibn Talib, May Allah (SWT) Be Pleased with them. There was also the brief period of leadership of Sayyidina Hasan ibn Ali (Ra). These blessed leaders have been regarded as 'rightly-guided' meaning they continued the leadership of the Ummah, by holding fast to the truth, and followed in the tradition of the Messenger ﷺ of Allah. The laws and traditions established in their era of leadership have remained till this day and have been universally accepted as being in accordance with the path of Sayyidina Rasulullah ﷺ (Salla lahu alayhi wa'ale hi Wasallam).

The Messenger ﷺ of Allah left behind nothing in *'dirham or dinar'*, meaning did not leave behind any wealth. The inheritance of the Messengers (Alayhimus Salaam) is considered *'sadaqah'* – charity. This is not even passed onto their heirs. The only inheritance of the Prophets is their knowledge. There are reasons why there is no material inheritance from the Prophets of Allah (SWT). The first is that the Prophets remain alive in their graves, and secondly the Prophets of Allah only possess what Allah (SWT) Bestows upon them to fulfil their basic needs, as caretakers. The sole purpose of the Prophets and Messengers, Peace be upon them all, to enter this world is to convey the Message of Allah (SWT). The blessed wives of Sayyidina Rasulullah ﷺ (Salla lahu alayhi wa'ale hi Wasallam) were prohibited to remarry in clear words in the Noble Qur'an.

'And it is not for you to cause annoyance to the Messenger ﷺ of Allah, nor that ye should ever marry his wives after him ﷺ. Lo! that in Allah's sight would be an enormity'.

(Al' Qur'an; 33:53)

Sayyidina Rasulullah ﷺ (Salla lahu alayhi wa'ale hi Wasallam) remains alive in his ﷺ blessed grave, as do all the Prophets of Allah. (Bayhaqi). The re-marrying of his ﷺ blessed wives, who Allah (SWT) Has Revealed as being the 'Mothers of the Believers', would cause pain to him ﷺ. This would not be acceptable to Allah (SWT).

Sayyidina Rasulullah ﷺ (Salla lahu alayhi wa'ale hi Wasallam) left behind a mule and some weapons. There was also a piece of land, and from its income, his ﷺ blessed family were supported. This land was not considered inheritance but was given as charity.

'Did We not Exalt you in your Fame'. **(Al Qur'an; 94:4)**

In the above verse, Allah (SWT) Mentions His favour upon Sayyidina Rasulullah ﷺ (Salla lahu alayhi wa'ale hi Wasallam). This favour is when Allah (SWT) Is Mentioned, His Final Messenger ﷺ will also be praised. The *Kalima*, and the *Adhaan* - Call to Prayer is proof of this.

Allah (SWT) confirmed to the Messenger ﷺ of Allah; 'When I am mentioned, you are mentioned with Me in this statement – *La illaha il Allah Muhammadur Rasulullah*. (Kitab' Ash-Shifa)

The blessings being sent upon Sayyidina Rasulullah ﷺ (Salla lahu alayhi wa'ale hi Wasallam) by his ﷺ Lord is continuous, and this is why Allah (SWT) Has Revealed in the Noble Qur'an that his ﷺ every moment will be better than the preceding one;

'And verily the latter portion will be better for thee than the former'.

(Al Qur'an; 93:4)

This is unique for the Messenger ﷺ of Allah, as Allah (SWT) elsewhere has Revealed that all of mankind is in a *'state of loss'* (103:2). However, for the Messenger ﷺ of Allah it has been revealed that his ﷺ every moment is better than the previous one.

Excellence of the Messenger ﷺ of Allah

'Lo! Allah and His angels shower blessings on the Prophet. O ye who believe! Ask blessings on him and salute him with a worthy salutation'.

(Al Qur'an; 94:4)

This above verse shows that Allah (SWT) is Blessing the Messenger ﷺ of Allah, with every moment that passes. His angels also send blessings upon the Messenger ﷺ, and Allah (SWT) has made it obligatory for all believers to send blessings upon Sayyidina Rasulullah ﷺ (Salla lahu alayhi wa'ale hi Wasallam).

Sayyidina Rasulullah ﷺ (Salla lahu alayhi wa'ale hi Wasallam) performed miracles – *mujizaat* at will through the permission of Allah (SWT), his ﷺ miracles transcended all the previous Prophets of Allah, Peace be upon them all.

The Messenger ﷺ of Allah, foretold future events and revealed past history, remaining consistent to his ﷺ Message, while bringing the most superior law for mankind. The *Shariah* given to Sayyidina Rasulullah ﷺ (Salla lahu alayhi wa'ale hi Wasallam) is superior to every law that preceded it, and the Messenger ﷺ of Allah was given the Final Revelation of Allah (SWT); 'Al Qur'an'.

The religion – *deen*, of the Messenger ﷺ of Allah, was given victory over all previous religions and many things were made permissible to his ﷺ Ummah – *Nation*, which were unlawful for previous nations. For example, the whole of the earth is a place of prayer for the followers of the Final Messenger ﷺ, on the condition the place is clean. Previous nations had been allocated specific places of prayer and were not permitted to pray elsewhere.

The Messenger ﷺ of Allah made lawful the pure things and unlawful the impure things and enforced through his ﷺ own infallible actions, the law of Islam. This law is still followed today and the authority of the Messenger ﷺ of Allah over the believers remains to this day and will continue until the end of time. Insha'Allah.

The law of Al'Qur'an, includes revelations of the 'Book of Psalms' - *'Zabur'*, 'The Torah' - *'Taurat'* and 'The Gospel' - *'Injil'*, yet is for the whole of mankind until the end of time. Previous books were only revealed for a certain time on a specific nation. The excellence of the Ummah of the Messenger ﷺ of Allah, is unquestioned and surpasses every other nation from the past. The scholars of the nation of the Messenger ﷺ of Allah have the honour of being like the Prophets (As) sent to *Bani Israel*; the Jewish nations, in knowledge only. This does not refer to the rank and honour of the Prophets of Allah, which cannot be reached by anyone who is not a Prophet. The generosity and piety of the followers of the Messenger ﷺ of Allah, surpassed all previous nations as they took their mercy from *'Rahmat lil Alamin'*; the Mercy onto the Worlds. This is one of the titles of the Messenger ﷺ of Allah, as revealed in the Noble Qur'an.

The followers of Sayyidina Eesa (Alayhi Salaam) - *Jesus* were following the laws as revealed in the 'Torah', upon the 'Bani Israel'. These teachings were perfected by the revelations given to Sayyidina Eesa (Alayhi Salaam), who was sent to re-establish that Law and Perfect the Word of Allah (SWT). Yet the followers of Sayyidina Rasulullah ﷺ (Salla lahu alayhi wa'ale hi Wasallam) had no previous text to follow, they were permitted only to follow the Noble Qur'an, which was revealed over a period of 23 years. Through these teachings the Companions (RadiyAllahu Anhumma) learnt of the previous Prophets of Allah, Peace be upon them, and the previous Books. However, they only believed in the teachings of the Messenger ﷺ of Allah, following his ﷺ *Sunnah* as being the Word of Allah (SWT). The Noble Qur'an was revealed over 23 years but the companions became

Muslims as soon as they believed in Allah (SWT) being 'Alone' in Worship, and by following the Messengership of Sayyidina Muhammad ﷺ ur Rasulullah (Salla lahu alayhi wa'ale hi Wasallam). This is the path of 'Ahl-e-Sunnah wal Jamaah' and will remain supreme till the final hour. The followers of Sayyidina Rasulullah ﷺ (Salla lahu alayhi wa'ale hi Wasallam) follow the teachings of the Qur'an and Sunnah; the guidance of the Ulama (Scholars); and the way of the Auliya; who are the Friends of Allah (SWT).

Every element of the life and legacy of the Messenger ﷺ of Allah is the Truth, his ﷺ example is supreme, and is without blemish or error. The Messenger ﷺ of Allah remained pure from all fault whether before or during the revelations. The perfection of character and conduct, physical form and spiritual state of the Final Messenger ﷺ, was witnessed by his ﷺ Companions (RadiyAllahu Anhumma); his enemies, and since by historians and scholars alike. Sayyidina Rasulullah ﷺ (Salla lahu alayhi wa'ale hi Wasallam) is the culmination of every quality of all the previous Prophets, Peace be upon them, in their every word and action, with their miracles and qualities. Allah (SWT) Protected His Final Messenger ﷺ (Salla lahu alayhi wa'ale hi Wasallam) from harm of hand and tongue, bestowing upon him ﷺ Divine Revelation, and Inspiration. The Messenger ﷺ of Allah, spoke the Word of Allah (SWT); the ultimate revelation upon mankind; *Al Qur'an*; in which Allah (SWT) Revealed that His Messenger ﷺ does not speak from his own caprice, but speaks from Divine Revelation. Aside from the Revealed verses, the Messenger ﷺ of Allah received inspiration, which became the *'Sunnah'*. This is the Path of the Messenger ﷺ of Allah, the second authentic point of reference after the Noble Qur'an.

Allah (SWT) Sent His Messenger ﷺ, adorned in some of His own attributes of *'Compassion'* and *'Mercy'*, to come from amongst us, but is not like us, in his ﷺ qualities or in reality.

(Kitab'Ash-Shifa)

The Messenger ﷺ of Allah said, *'I am the master of the children of Adam, and I am not proud'*.

(Sahih Muslim / Jami Tirmidhi)

PART II – THE PROPHETIC ATTRIBUTES

Introduction

Allah (SWT) Has not Bestowed so many of His own attributes to any of His creation, aside from Sayyidina Muhammad ﷺ (Salla lahu alayhi wa'ale hi Wasallam). However the Attributes of Allah (SWT) Are Infinite, and are among the Divine Qualities of Allah (SWT), and those attributed to His Final Messenger ﷺ, are gifts from Allah (SWT), in the Reality that only He Knows.

The attributes of beauty; lineage; good conduct; intellect; are among those that are praiseworthy, even if found in lesser amounts in any human being. Yet in the Messenger ﷺ of Allah, these qualities were present to the highest degree, without fault or error. The beauty of Sayyidina Rasulullah ﷺ (Salla lahu alayhi wa'ale hi Wasallam) was such that it became a proof of his ﷺ prophethood, and was regarded as among his ﷺ miracles. Beauty inspires awe, and the awe of Sayyidina Rasulullah ﷺ (Salla lahu alayhi wa'ale hi Wasallam) was equivalent to a distance of a month. This is an Arab proverb, which means its impact would be felt for the distance travelled in a month. Having the best lineage, was among the signs of Prophethood, and all the Prophets who preceded him ﷺ, were blessed with the best lineage. The mannerisms of Sayyidina Rasulullah ﷺ (Salla lahu alayhi wa'ale hi Wasallam) were cloaked in humility, and modesty. The Messenger ﷺ of Allah, remained constant in action, never deviating from the Message, or the Example. Such steadfastness in action, can only be found in someone who is inspired through Divine Inspiration. Similarly, the intellect is found to be natural but can be enhanced by education and tutelage. Yet, Sayyidina Rasulullah ﷺ (Salla lahu alayhi wa'ale hi Wasallam) was raised as an orphan, by relatives, and was a tradesman, with limited access to foreign cultures. However the intellect of Sayyidina Rasulullah ﷺ (Salla lahu alayhi wa'ale hi Wasallam), far exceeded the most literate of his ﷺ time.

The Arab culture was proud of its orators, who could mesmerise others through poetic excellence, and unparalleled rhetoric. Sayyidina Rasulullah ﷺ (Salla lahu alayhi wa'ale hi Wasallam) left even the most learned speechless, through knowledge of previous nations, and a deep understanding of local cultures. The speech of Sayyidina Rasulullah ﷺ (Salla lahu alayhi wa'ale hi Wasallam) was eloquent beyond reproach, and upon it came the ultimate Word of Allah (SWT).

This section has been partly inspired from the writings of Harun Yahya. However it has been complimented by authentic narrations from highly acclaimed books, such as *'Ash'aam'il Muhammidiyyah* ﷺ', as compiled by Imam Tirmidhi (Rahmatullah Alayh), and *'Kitab' Ash-Shifa'* authored by Imam Qadi Iyad (Rahmatullah Alayh). Here we discuss some of the attributes bestowed upon the Messenger ﷺ of Allah, of beauty, lineage, compassion, humility, strength, patience, and honour, among many. These are the apparent qualities of Sayyidina Rasulullah ﷺ, which were so abundant that they could not have been present in one human being, without this being a Miracle of Allah (SWT).

The qualities found in any human being, are either inherited, or are acquired. The attributes of having a good lineage, physical beauty; soundness of intellect; eloquence; honour of birthplace, are all natural, and cannot be acquired through a person's own endeavour. (Ash-Shifa). Even qualities such as courage and patience, are considered natural, yet some believe a person can acquire them through being steadfast. Other qualities such as being knowledgeable; generous, thankful; just; humble; fearing Allah (SWT); and being merciful, can be established within a person, through dedication and sacrifice. Same can be said for being an ascetic, as this comes from giving up the love of this world. Imam Qadi Iyaad (Rh) discusses that if the best of all qualities, whether those that could only be naturally present, along with all the attributes that can be acquired through steadfastness, are all found in such great abundance, within the same human being, then such a person would be a living miracle. A human being would not be able to attain such great distinction through their own disposition. This is why the attributes of Sayyidina Rasulullah ﷺ (Salla lahu alayhi wa'ale hi Wasallam) were among his ﷺ miracles. The Messenger ﷺ of Allah was Bestowed with such praiseworthy qualities that those who went to him ﷺ as enemies, fell at his ﷺ blessed feet. Even the enemies of the Messenger ﷺ of Allah would be unable to utter a word against him ﷺ when asked to, and his ﷺ companions willingly gave up their every breathe for him ﷺ.

Here we discuss some of these immeasurable qualities, yet as the scholars discuss that what we witness are his ﷺ 'attributes'; his ﷺ 'qualities', by which we would know him ﷺ, and know the Message. However the reality, the truth of him ﷺ; the *'Haqiqah ul' Muhammidiyah* ﷺ' is something else, and has not been revealed upon mankind. The 'Muhammadan ﷺ Reality' far exceeds his ﷺ physical form, and visible signs. It is only known by Allah (SWT).

The Beauty of the Messenger ﷺ of Allah

It has been narrated by Sayyidina Ibrahim ibn Muhammad (RadiyAllahu Anhu), one of the grandchildren of Sayyidina Ali ibn Abi Talib (RadiyAllahu Anhu):

"One who strove to convey his ﷺ superior traits and impressive qualities simply confessed his inability and incompetence in describing him ﷺ by stating that he has never before him ﷺ or after him ﷺ seen anyone comparable to him ﷺ".

(Harun Yahya)

The narrations discussing the beauty of the form of the Messenger ﷺ of Allah, are available in such a great number that they could be compiled in many volumes. Beauty in itself is a praiseworthy quality, and brings awe to those in its present. Here we include some of these narrations, which describe the mesmerising physical form of Sayyidina Rasulullah ﷺ (Salla lahu alayhi wa'ale hi Wasallam).

The Messenger ﷺ of Allah, had the most radiant complexion, described as being fair with tints of reddish colouring, deep eyes with perfect black pupils; his ﷺ blessed eyelashes were long. Sayyidina Rasulullah ﷺ (Salla lahu alayhi wa'ale hi Wasallam) had a blessed round face, likened to the full moon; his ﷺ skin was smooth; and the beard of the Messenger ﷺ of Allah was thick and dense. The blessed hair of the Messenger ﷺ of Allah was longer than those that reached the earlobes, and shorter than those that reached the shoulders.

The blessed neck of the Messenger ﷺ of Allah was beautiful and thin, and if the rays of the sun fell on his ﷺ blessed neck, it appeared like a cup of silver mixed with gold. The blessed stomach and chest were perfectly in line. Sayyidina Rasulullah ﷺ (Salla lahu alayhi wa'ale hi Wasallam) had large joints, with wide chest and shoulders. The blessed teeth of the Messenger ﷺ of Allah were white as pearls, and when the Messenger ﷺ smiled, a light reflected from them.

Sayyidina Baraa bin Aazib (RadiyAllahu Anhu) relates that: "Sayyidina Rasulullah ﷺ (Salla lahu alayhi wa'ale hi Wasallam) was a man of a medium build; with broad shoulders; had dense hair which reached their ear-lobes. Sayyidina Rasulullah ﷺ (Salla lahu alayhi wa'ale hi Wasallam) wore a red striped izzar (a cloth worn around the legs) and shawl. "I never saw anybody or anything more handsome than Sayyidina Rasulullah ﷺ (Salla lahu alayhi wa'ale hi Wasallam)".

(Ash'aam-il Muhammidiyah ﷺ)

It is related from Sayyidina Jaabir (RadiyAllahu Anhu) that he said: " I once saw Sayyidina Rasulullah ﷺ (Salla lahu alayhi wa'ale hi Wasallam) on the night of a full moon. On that night Sayyidina Rasulullah ﷺ (Salla lahu alayhi wa'ale hi Wasallam) wore red clothing. At times I looked at the full moon and at times at Sayyidina Rasulullah ﷺ (Salla lahu alayhi wa'ale hi Wasallam). Ultimately I came to the conclusion that Sayyidina Rasulullah ﷺ (Salla lahu alayhi wa'ale hi Wasallam) was more handsome, beautiful and more radiant than the full moon."

(Ash'aam-il Muhammidiyah ﷺ)

It is related from Sayyidina Ebrahim bin Muhammad (RadiyAllahu Anhu) who is from the sons (grandsons) of Sayyidina Ali ibn Abi Talib (RadiyAllahu Anhu), that whenever Sayyidina Ali ibn Abi Talib (RadiyAllahu Anhu) described the noble features of Sayyidina Rasulullah ﷺ (Salla lahu alayhi wa'ale hi Wasallam), he would say:

"Sayyidina Rasulullah ﷺ (Salla lahu alayhi wa'ale hi Wasallam) was neither very tall nor short, but of a medium stature among people. His ﷺ blessed hair was neither very curly nor very straight, but had a slight wave in it.

Sayyidina Rasulullah ﷺ (Salla lahu alayhi wa'ale hi Wasallam) did not have a big body nor a round face, but their blessed face was slightly round (meaning did not have a fully round face nor a fully elongated face, but in between the two).

The complexion of Sayyidina Rasulullah ﷺ (Salla lahu alayhi wa'ale hi Wasallam) was white with redness in it.

The blessed eyes of Sayyidina Rasulullah ﷺ (Salla lahu alayhi wa'ale hi Wasallam) were extremely black. His ﷺ eyelashes were long. The joints of his ﷺ blessed body were large, likewise the portion between the two shoulders was broad and fully fleshed. There was no hair (more than normal) on their blessed body. (Some people have profuse hair on their body. Sayyidina Rasulullah ﷺ (Salla lahu alayhi wa'ale hi Wasallam) did not have hair on the parts of their blessed body, besides places like the arms and legs etc.).

Sayyidina Rasulullah ﷺ (Salla lahu alayhi wa'ale hi Wasallam) had a thin line of hair running from their chest to the navel. The hands and feet of Sayyidina Rasulullah ﷺ (Salla lahu alayhi wa'ale hi Wasallam) were fully fleshed.

Sayyidina Rasulullah ﷺ (Salla lahu alayhi wa'ale hi Wasallam) walked and would lift their blessed legs with vigour, as if descending from a higher place.

Any person who saw Sayyidina Rasulullah ﷺ (Salla lahu alayhi wa'ale hi Wasallam) suddenly would become awe-inspired.

Sayyidina Rasulullah ﷺ (Salla lahu alayhi wa'ale hi Wasallam) had such a great personality and dignity, that the person who saw him ﷺ for the first time, because of that awe-inspiring personality, would be overcome with a feeling of profound respect.

Firstly, there is an awe- rau`b for physical beauty, and addition to this, when other perfection- kamaalat are added what more could then be said of the awe of Sayyidina Rasulullah ﷺ (Salla lahu alayhi wa'ale hi Wasallam). Subhan-Allah – Glory belongs to Allah.

Besides, the special attributes and qualities granted to Sayyidina Rasulullah ﷺ (Salla lahu alayhi wa'ale hi Wasallam), awe is one of the special qualities granted. Anyone who came in close contact with Sayyidina Rasulullah ﷺ (Salla lahu alayhi wa'ale hi Wasallam), and knew his ﷺ excellent character was smitten with the love of his ﷺ excellent attributes. Anyone who described his ﷺ noble features can only say: *"I have not seen anyone like Sayyidina Rasulullah ﷺ (Salla lahu alayhi wa'ale hi Wasallam) neither before nor after him ﷺ."*

(Ash'aam-il Muhammidiyah ﷺ)

The Pleasant Scent of the Messenger ﷺ of Allah

Sayyidina Jaabir bin Samura (RadiyAllahu Anhu) states: "Whenever the Prophet ﷺ of Allah, had been on a particular pathway, when someone passed by later, they could recognize that the Prophet ﷺ had passed by there because of his ﷺ scent."

(Sahih Bukhari)

The blessed body of the Messenger ﷺ of Allah is free from anything impure. This is why the perspiration of Sayyidina Rasulullah ﷺ (Salla lahu alayhi wa'ale hi Wasallam), had the most beautiful scent, and was used to *perfume* the perfume. Narrations confirm that the blessed wives of the Messenger ﷺ of Allah, would gather droplets of the perspiration of the Messenger ﷺ of Allah, and would collect them in a small bottle. Some of the narrations regarding the scent of the Messenger ﷺ of Allah, are included here.

Sayyidina Jaabir ibn Samura (RadiyAllahu Anhu) has mentioned that the 'Messenger ﷺ of Allah touched his cheek, and he said, 'I felt a cool sensation from the scent of his ﷺ hand. It was as though the Messenger ﷺ of Allah had placed his ﷺ hand in a bag of perfume'.

(Sahih Muslim)

Sayyidina Rasulullah ﷺ (Salla lahu alayhi wa'ale hi Wasallam) slept on a rug in the house of Sayyidina Anas ibn Malik (RadiyAllahu Anhu), who narrates that his mother would collect the blessed perspiration of the Messenger ﷺ of Allah in a long-necked bottle. Sayyidina Anas Ibn Malik (Ra) said, 'The Messenger ﷺ of Allah asked her about this, and she replied, 'We put it in our perfume, and it is the most fragrant of scents'.

(Sahih Bukhari / Sahih Muslim)

A beautiful narration has been mentioned by the great Wali of Allah (SWT), the great Muhaddith (Compiler of Hadith); Shah Abdul Haq Muhaddith Dehlavi (Rahmatullah Alayh), in which he writes that a man was in search of a perfume, on the occasion of his daughter's wedding. He did not find a scent pleasant enough, to gift his daughter. This person presented himself in the gathering of Sayyidina Rasulullah ﷺ (Salla lahu alayhi wa'ale hi Wasallam). He explained this to the Messenger ﷺ of Allah, who requested that a small bottle be brought to him ﷺ. The Messenger ﷺ of Allah placed droplets of his ﷺ own perspiration in the container, and presented it to this man. The man took this to his daughter, and instructed her to apply this on the day of her wedding. On the day of her wedding, Medina t'ul Munnawarah was engulfed in the beautiful scent of this perfume, and this man's house was named; *'Bait'ul Muttayyabain'*. Meaning the 'House of Scent'.

It has been mentioned that this bride never needed to apply any perfume for the rest of her life, and this beautiful fragrance of Sayyidina Rasulullah ﷺ (Salla lahu alayhi wa'ale hi Wasallam) emanated from her, and even from every child from her family, for many generations that followed.

(Al Burhan Sharif)

The Lineage of the Messenger ﷺ of Allah

Among the signs of the excellence of the Messenger ﷺ of Allah, include his ﷺ noble lineage, and place of birth. The purity of the ancestors of Sayyidina Rasulullah ﷺ (Salla lahu alayhi wa'ale hi Wasallam), assured the purity of his ﷺ heritage. The Messenger ﷺ of Allah said that,

'Allah brought me down to earth in the loins of Adam (Alayhi Salaam), placed me in the loins of Nuh (Alayhi Salaam), then cast me into the loins of Ibrahim (Alayhi Salaam). Allah (SWT) Moved me from noble loins and pure wombs, until I reached my parents. None of my ancestors were ever joined together in fornication. All of them were brought together in lawful marriage'.

(Kitab'Ash-Shifa)

Sayyidina Rasulullah ﷺ (Salla lahu alayhi wa'ale hi Wasallam) was the best of the sons of Banu Hashim. The clan of Banu Hashim was the best of the tribe of Quraysh, who were the best of the tribe of Banu Kinana, and they were the best of the sons of Sayyidina Isma'il (Alayhi Salaam). The narrations included in this section mention the excellence of the lineage of the Messenger ﷺ of Allah;

Sayyidina Abu Hurayra (RadiyAllahu Anhu) mentions that, 'The Messenger ﷺ of Allah said, 'I have been sent from the best of each generation of the children of Adam (As), generation after generation, until I was placed in the generation from which I came'.

(Sahih Bukhari)

Sayyidina Al-Abbas (RadiyAllahu Anhu) said that the Prophet ﷺ said, 'Allah Placed me in the Best of Creation, selecting the best of them from the best of their generations; then selected the Best tribes from among them; then selected the Best families among them; and I am the Best of them, in person, and in lineage'.

(Tirmidhi)

A further clarification of this hadith is mentioned, as narrated by Sayyidina Wa'ila ibn al-Aqsa (Ra), who narrated that the Messenger ﷺ of Allah said,

'Allah (SWT) Chose Isma'il (Alayhi Salaam) from the children of Ibrahim (Alayhi Salaam), and chose Banu Kinana from the offspring of Sayyidina Isma'il (As). From them, the tribe of Quraysh was chosen, and Banu Hashim as the best of them. I am the best of the sons of Banu Hashim'.

(Kitab'Ash-Shifa)

The place of birth of Sayyidina Rasulullah ﷺ (Salla lahu alayhi wa'ale hi Wasallam), is the best of all cities. Makka t'ul Makkaramah. This city was established for the sole purpose of Worshipping Allah (SWT) since the time of Sayyidina Adam (Alayhi Salaam). The place where the Messenger ﷺ of Allah migrated to was Medina t'ul Munnawarah, in which is one of the gardens of Paradise - *Al Jannah*.

Allah (SWT) took Oath by His Beloved Prophet ﷺ, several times in the Noble Qur'an. Including on the place in which the Messenger ﷺ of Allah resides;

'I Swear by this land, and you are a habitant of this land'.

(Al' Qur'an; 90:1-2)

Al Wasiti (Rh) included in his commentary that, 'Allah (SWT) is saying, *'We swear to you by this land which He Honoured by the fact that the Messenger ﷺ of Allah lived there'*.

Some commentaries state this land refers to Medina. However Imam Qadi Iyad (Rh) believes it is Makka.

(Ash-Shifa)

The Humility of the Messenger ﷺ of Allah

Narrated by Sayyidina Imam Hasan ibn Ali (RadiyAllahu Anhu): "Our Messenger ﷺ of Allah, was, by nature, imposing and magnificent."

(Harun Yahya)

The blessed companions; Sayyidina Abu Dharr; Sayyidina Ibn Umar; Sayyidina Ibn Abbas; Sayyidina Abu Hurayrah; and Sayyidina Jabir ibn Abdullah, May Allah (SWT) Be Pleased with them, all relate that the Messenger ﷺ of Allah said,

'I have been given five things, which no Prophet before me has been given; I have been assisted with awe being cast into the hearts of my enemies a month in advance of my arrival; The earth has been made a place of worship for me, and a place of purity, so that when the time of prayer comes, a person of my community can pray within; The bounty of war, which was not lawful for any Prophet before me, has been made lawful for me; I have been sent to the whole of Mankind; I have been given intercession'.

(Ash-Shifa by Qadi Iyad (Rh))

Sayyidina Uqba ibn Amir (RadiyAllahu Anhu) narrates that Sayyidina Rasulullah ﷺ (Salla lahu alayhi wa'ale hi Wasallam) said, 'I will go ahead on your behalf, and I will be a witness for you. By Allah, I am looking at the Water-Basin even now. I have been given the keys to the treasures of the earth. By Allah, I do not fear that you will associate anything with Allah, after me, but I fear that you will contend with each other for this world'.

(Ibid)

In the 'Musnad' of Imam Ahmed ibn Hanbal (Rahmatullah Alayh), a hadith is found, narrated by Sayyidina Abdullah Ibn Amr (RadiyAllahu Anhu), who relates that;

The Messenger ﷺ of Allah said, 'I am Muhammad, the Unlettered Prophet ﷺ. There is no Prophet after me. I was given all the words and their seals. I was made to recognize the Guardians of the Fire; and the Bearers of the Throne'.

(Musnad Ahmed)

The above narrations emphasise the tremendous honour bestowed upon Sayyidina Rasulullah ﷺ (Salla lahu alayhi wa'ale hi Wasallam). It is mentioned through authentic narrations, that the Messenger ﷺ of Allah informed his ﷺ blessed companions of his ﷺ unique qualities, and the fact that Allah (SWT) Bestowed upon him ﷺ, all the marvels of the seen and unseen worlds. In fact, the magnitude of this cannot even be comprehended by us, as we are restricted by our limited intellect. Also, the Messenger ﷺ of Allah, informed us that we will not commit the major sin of Shirk, which is to associate anything with Allah (SWT), but will begin to compete for the riches of this world. This is something we are seeing today.

The purpose of beginning this section on the humility of Sayyidina Rasulullah ﷺ (Salla lahu alayhi wa'ale hi Wasallam), with the above narrations, is to demonstrate how despite being honoured with the sublime qualities of Prophethood; Seal of Messengership; knowledge of the unseen; being a witness for mankind; and unlimited qualities of beauty; and heritage, the Messenger ﷺ of Allah remained the most humble, and grateful. A person would easily succumb to becoming proud; even when granted the least of qualities, or being praised moderately, yet the Messenger ﷺ of Allah displayed the degree of humility, which could not be present in a normal human being. The narrations below are examples of this;

Allah (SWT) gave the choice to His beloved Messenger ﷺ, to be Granted a Kingdom, like that of Sayyidina Sulayman ibn Daawud (Alayhi Salaam) – *King Solomon*, or be a humble *Abd*; Slave of Allah. The Messenger ﷺ of Allah chose the latter.

(Qadi Iyad)

A man came to the Messenger ﷺ of Allah, and began to tremble out of awe of him ﷺ. The Messenger ﷺ of Allah comforted him, saying, 'I am not a king, I am the son of a Qurayshi lady, who ate dried meat'.

(Ash-Shifa)

In another narration, the Messenger ﷺ of Allah, said, 'I am a slave. I eat as a slave eats; and I sit as a slave sits'.

(Ash-Shifa)

Sayyidina Anas (RadiyAllahu Anhu) reports: "A woman came to Sayyidina Rasulullah ﷺ (Salla lahu alayhi wa'ale hi Wasallam) and said: 'I would like to speak to you in private'. Sayyidina Rasulullah ﷺ (Salla lahu alayhi wa'ale hi Wasallam) replied: 'Sit on any street of Medina and I will come there and listen to you' ".

(This woman was known as someone not mentally stable, who people would ignore. Yet the Messenger ﷺ of Allah gave her his ﷺ complete attention).

(Tirmidhi)

Sayyidina Anas (RadiyAllahu Anhu) reports: "Sayyidina Rasulullah ﷺ (Salla lahu alayhi wa'ale hi Wasallam) visited the sick, attended funerals, rode on donkeys, accepted the invitations of slaves. On the day of the 'Battle of Banu Qurayzah', Sayyidina Rasulullah ﷺ (Salla lahu alayhi wa'ale hi Wasallam) rode on a donkey, the reigns of which were made of date palm leaves. On it was also a saddle made of date palm leaves".

(Ash'aam-il)

Sayyidina Amrah (RadiyAllahu Anha) reports that someone asked Sayyidina Aayeshaa Siddiqua (RadiyAllahu Anha). "What was the normal practice of Sayyidina Rasulullah ﷺ (Salla lahu alayhi wa'ale hi Wasallam) at home"? Sayyidina Aayeshaa Siddiqua (RadiyAllahu Anha) replied: "Sayyidina Rasulullah ﷺ (Salla lahu alayhi wa'ale hi Wasallam) was a human from among other humans. Sayyidina Rasulullah ﷺ (Salla lahu alayhi wa'ale hi Wasallam) himself removed the lice from his ﷺ blessed clothing, milked his ﷺ goats, and did all his ﷺ work himself".

(Ash'aam-il)

Sayyidina Ayeshaa Siddiqua (RadiyAllahu Anha); Sayyidina Hasan ibn Ali (RadiyAllahu Anhu); Sayyidina Abu Sa'id al-Khudri (RadiyAllahu Anhu), have all narrated, the Messenger ﷺ of Allah would work in the house with his ﷺ family, would tend to his ﷺ own clothes and sweep the house. The Messenger ﷺ of Allah would take his ﷺ camels to graze, and would eat with his ﷺ servants. The Messenger ﷺ of Allah would knead bread, and would carry his ﷺ own goods from the marketplace'.

(Ash-Shifa)

On the conquest of Makka, as the Messenger ﷺ of Allah entered as the victor, his ﷺ blessed head was lowered, to such an extent that nearly touched the front saddle, out of his ﷺ humility to Allah (SWT).

(Qadi Iyad)

The Sublime Manner of the Messenger ﷺ of Allah

As narrated by Sayyidina Hasan ibn Ali, from his blessed father; Sayyidina Ali ibn Abi Talib, May Allah (SWT) Be Pleased with them;

"The Messenger ﷺ of Allah. was the one who smiled the most and the most joyful of all."

(Tirmidhi)

The manner of Sayyidina Rasulullah ﷺ (Salla lahu alayhi wa'ale hi Wasallam) was one of simplicity, and humility. The Messenger ﷺ of Allah did not indulge in any excessiveness, and preferred to be without excess means, and do with very little. This was despite the fact that Allah (SWT) Revealed that the Messenger ﷺ of Allah could have the Mountains of Makka turned into gold, yet the Messenger ﷺ preferred a life of abstinence, to be given food to eat one day, in order to be thankful, and to be without the next day, in order to be patient.

(Sahih Bukhari)

Another quality of the manner in which the Messenger ﷺ of Allah lived, was to act like others, and not expect special treatment, or become aloof, as is often the case with leaders and kings. The tremendous love and respect that the Companions, May Allah (SWT) Be Pleased with them, had was out of the awe of his ﷺ blessed personality, and not out of fear or need. Below are some of the narrations that explain how the Messenger ﷺ of Allah lived;

Sayyidina Qaylah bint Makhramah (RadiyAllahu Anhu) reports; 'I saw the Messenger ﷺ of Allah in the Masjid (in a very humble posture) sitting. Due to his ﷺ awe-inspiring personality, I began shivering.'

(Ash-Shifa)

Sayyidina Maalik bin Dinaar (RadiyAllahu Anhu) says: "Sayyidina Rasulullah ﷺ (Salla lahu alayhi wa'ale hi Wasallam) never filled his ﷺ blessed stomach with meat and bread, except at the time of <u>d</u>*afaf*. I asked a badawi. 'What does <u>d</u>afaf mean?' He replied: 'It is to eat together with people".

(Tirmidhi)

This means that the Messenger ﷺ of Allah, would always choose hunger, except when being part of a gathering. In these situations, the Messenger ﷺ of Allah would ensure the guests ate satisfactorily by participating with them. This also shows the blessed manner of the Messenger ﷺ of Allah, by not appearing different from the others, and also establishes the *Sunnah* of being a good host, and guest.

Sayyidina Aayeshaa Siddiqua (RadiyAllahu Anha) reports: "We the family of Sayyidina Muhammad ﷺ (Salla lahu alayhi wa'ale hi Wasallam) did not light a fire for months in our homes. We sustained ourselves on dates and water".

(Tirmidhi)

Sayyidina Anas (RadiyAllahu Anhu) reports that a tailor invited Sayyidina Rasulullah ﷺ (Salla lahu alayhi wa'ale hi Wasallam). <u>Th</u>areed was served, in which *'dubbaa'* – pumpkin was added. Sayyidina Rasulullah ﷺ (Salla lahu alayhi wa'ale hi Wasallam) liked dubbaa so began eating it. Sayyidina Anas (RadiyAllahu Anhu) says: "After that no food was prepared for me, wherein if gourd could be added, it was always added".

(Ash'aam-il)

Sayyidina Anas (RadiyAllahu Anhu) also reports that the Messenger ﷺ of Allah, would be invited to eat barley bread, and would accept the invitation.

(Ash-Shifa)

Sayyidina Nu'maan ibn Bashir (RadiyAllahu Anhu) stated, after the passing of the Messenger ﷺ of Allah, "Are you not in the luxuries of eating and drinking, whereas, I had observed that Sayyidina Rasulullah ﷺ (Salla lahu alayhi wa'ale hi Wasallam) did not possess ordinary types of dates to fill his ﷺ blessed stomach".

(Tirmidhi)

Sayyidina Nofal bin Iyaas Al Hadhali (RadiyAllahu Anhu) says "'Sayyidina Abdurrahmaan bin 'Awf (RadiyAllahu Anhu) (who is a Sahaabi from among the 'Ashrah Mubash-sharah' *(Companions who were promised Paradise in their lifetime))* was an associate of ours, and verily he was the best associate. Once we were returning from a place with him. On returning we went with him to his house. When he went home he first took a bath. After he had taken a bath, bread and meat was brought in a big utensil. Upon seeing this Sayyidina Abdurrahmaan (RadiyAllahu Anhu) began to cry. I asked: 'What happened, why are you crying'? He began saying: 'Till the passing of Sayyidina Rasulullah ﷺ (Salla lahu alayhi wa'ale hi Wasallam), nor did Sayyidina Rasulullah ﷺ (Salla lahu alayhi wa'ale hi Wasallam), nor his ﷺ blessed family members (RadiyAllahu Anhum) ever fill their stomachs even if it was only with bread made of barley. Now after Sayyidina Rasulullah ﷺ (Salla lahu alayhi wa'ale hi Wasallam), as far as I can think, this wealthy status of ours is not for any good'.

(Ash'aam-il)

Sayyidina Aayeshaa Siddiqua (RadiyAllahu Anha) reports that the bed on which Sayyidina Rasulullah ﷺ (Salla lahu alayhi wa'ale hi Wasallam) slept was made of leather, in which was filled coir of the palm tree.

(Ash'aam-il)

The narration of Sayyidina Hasan ibn Ali (RadiyAllahu Anhu) is among the most famous, on the manner of the Messenger ﷺ of Allah. It is based on what was narrated by Sayyidina Imam Hussain (RadiyAllahu Anhu), from their father. I have included parts of this narration below;

Sayyidina Imaam Hasan (RadiyAllahu Anhu) says, (my younger brother) Sayyidina Imaam Hussain (RadiyAllahu Anhu) said: "I asked my father (Sayyidina Ali ibn Abi Talib (RadiyAllahu Anhu)) about the conduct of Sayyidina Rasulullah ﷺ (Salla lahu alayhi wa'ale hi Wasallam) in his ﷺ blessed assemblies;

Sayyidina Ali ibn Abi Talib (RadiyAllahu Anhu) replied: 'Sayyidina Rasulullah ﷺ (Salla lahu alayhi wa'ale hi Wasallam) was always happy and easy mannered. There was always a smile and a sign of happiness on his ﷺ blessed face.

Sayyidina Rasulullah ﷺ was soft-natured and when the people needed his ﷺ approval, Sayyidina Rasulullah ﷺ (Salla lahu alayhi wa'ale hi Wasallam) easily gave consent.

Sayyidina Rasulullah ﷺ (Salla lahu alayhi wa'ale hi Wasallam) did not speak in a harsh tone nor was Sayyidina Rasulullah ﷺ (Salla lahu alayhi wa'ale hi Wasallam) stone-hearted.

Sayyidina Rasulullah ﷺ (Salla lahu alayhi wa'ale hi Wasallam) did not raise his ﷺ voice while speaking, nor was rude or spoke indecently.

Sayyidina Rasulullah ﷺ (Salla lahu alayhi wa'ale hi Wasallam) did not seek to point out other's faults.

Sayyidina Rasulullah ﷺ (Salla lahu alayhi wa'ale hi Wasallam) never overpraised anything, nor exceeded in joking, and Sayyidina Rasulullah ﷺ (Salla lahu alayhi wa'ale hi Wasallam) was not a miser.

Sayyidina Rasulullah ﷺ (Salla lahu alayhi wa'ale hi Wasallam) kept away from undesirable language and did not make as if not hearing something.

If Sayyidina Rasulullah ﷺ (Salla lahu alayhi wa'ale hi Wasallam) did not agree with the next person's wish, Sayyidina Rasulullah ﷺ (Salla lahu alayhi wa'ale hi Wasallam) did not make that person feel disheartened, nor made any false promise to that person.

Sayyidina Rasulullah ﷺ (Salla lahu alayhi wa'ale hi Wasallam) kept himself ﷺ away from three things: arguments, pride and senseless utterances.

Sayyidina Rasulullah ﷺ (Salla lahu alayhi wa'ale hi Wasallam) prohibited people from these things. Sayyidina Rasulullah ﷺ (Salla lahu alayhi wa'ale hi Wasallam) did not disgrace or insult anyone, nor look for the faults of others.

Sayyidina Rasulullah ﷺ (Salla lahu alayhi wa'ale hi Wasallam) only spoke that from which *thwaab* - reward was attained.

When Sayyidina Rasulullah ﷺ (Salla lahu alayhi wa'ale hi Wasallam) spoke, those present bowed their heads in such a manner, as if birds were sitting on their heads. (They did not shift about, as if birds will fly away on the slightest movement).

When Sayyidina Rasulullah ﷺ (Salla lahu alayhi wa'ale hi Wasallam) finished talking, the others would begin speaking. (No one would speak while Sayyidina Rasulullah ﷺ (Salla lahu alayhi wa'ale hi Wasallam) was speaking.

When we all laughed at something, Sayyidina Rasulullah ﷺ (Salla lahu alayhi wa'ale hi Wasallam) would smile too. The things that surprised others, Sayyidina Rasulullah ﷺ (Salla lahu alayhi wa'ale hi Wasallam) would also show surprise regarding that. (Sayyidina Rasulullah ﷺ (Salla lahu alayhi wa'ale hi Wasallam) would not sit quietly and keep himself ﷺ aloof from everyone, but made himself ﷺ part of the gathering).

Sayyidina Rasulullah ﷺ (Salla lahu alayhi wa'ale hi Wasallam) displayed patience at the harshness and indecent questions of a traveller. (Travellers would often lack courtesy when asking questions. Sayyidina Rasulullah ﷺ (Salla lahu alayhi wa'ale hi Wasallam) did not reprimand them but exercised patience).

(Tirmidhi)

The Food of the Messenger ﷺ of Allah

The blessed way of Sayyidina Rasulullah ﷺ (Salla lahu alayhi wa'ale hi Wasallam) is to only eat what is necessary for the body to remain healthy. Eating should not be excessive, as filling the stomach dulls the intellect, and makes a person neglectful of worship. It has been mentioned in the narrations, the Messenger ﷺ of Allah said,

'Sufficient for the son of Adam, are some morsels to keep his back straight'.

(Ash-Shifa)

In this section, there are narrations included in regard to the food that was preferred by the Messenger ﷺ of Allah, who would never over-praise food, or criticize food. This section compliments the narrations included in the previous section.

Upon visiting the poor, Sayyidina Rasulullah ﷺ (Salla lahu alayhi wa'ale hi Wasallam) praised vinegar. Vinegar is eaten with bread and this is described as the best combination. Vinegar is good for the poor. Also there are many diseases that are caused by excessive acid in the stomach, vinegar can relieve this. Modern study shows that one spoon of vinegar every day can prevent cancer. It is a blessed practice to eat vinegar every evening.

Dates were eaten by Sayyidina Rasulullah ﷺ (Salla lahu alayhi wa'ale hi Wasallam). The Companions (RadiyAllahu Anhum) would say Sayyidina Rasulullah ﷺ (Salla lahu alayhi wa'ale hi Wasallam) until passing away, never had enough dry dates at any time.

Meat is amongst the food eaten by Sayyidina Rasulullah ﷺ (Salla lahu alayhi wa'ale hi Wasallam). The Messenger ﷺ of Allah would eat lamb meat, especially the foreshank part, which is the top of the front leg of the sheep. Sayyidina Rasulullah ﷺ (Salla lahu alayhi wa'ale hi Wasallam) would also eat the arm of the lamb, neck of the lamb and part of the chest of the lamb. Narrations confirm that Sayyidina Rasulullah ﷺ (Salla lahu alayhi wa'ale hi Wasallam) would eat dried meat. It is known that the poor people eat dried meat.

Once a lady came to Sayyidina Rasulullah ﷺ (Salla lahu alayhi wa'ale hi Wasallam) and she was shaking in awe of the blessed presence of the Messenger ﷺ of Allah. On seeing this, Sayyidina Rasulullah ﷺ (Salla lahu alayhi wa'ale hi Wasallam) stated to her that she should not worry as *'I am born from a woman in Quraysh who used to eat dried meat'*.

(Ash-Shifa)

To eat sweet food is amongst the *Sunnah* of the Messenger ﷺ of Allah. Sayyidina Rasulullah ﷺ (Salla lahu alayhi wa'ale hi Wasallam) loved to eat 'halwa' and 'honey'. Both 'halwa' and 'honey' are good for energy and digestion. The scholars confirm they are beneficial to the body, along with meat.

Olive Oil, has numerous benefits, and traditions confirm that Sayyidina Rasulullah ﷺ (Salla lahu alayhi wa'ale hi Wasallam) ate olive oil and also applied it on their blessed hair. This oil has come from a blessed tree. The Olive tree has great barakha – *blessings,* and it is the first tree that grew after the flood of Sayyidina Nuh (Alayhi Salaam) – *Prophet Noah.*

(Ash'aam-il)

Pumpkin, was amongst the food that Sayyidina Rasulullah ﷺ (Salla lahu alayhi wa'ale hi Wasallam) loved to eat. Pumpkins have great benefit to the stomach and the abdomen. They also strengthen the mind and increase the IQ.

The manner in which Sayyidina Rasulullah ﷺ ate, was not to be comfortable, but to be sitting in a posture to limit the consumption of food. The companions (RadiyAllahu Anhumma) mentioned that the Messenger ﷺ of Allah would sit in the manner to eat, as though getting ready to leave at any moment.

(Sahih Muslim)

Sayyidina Abu Juhayfah (RadiyAllahu Anhu) says: "Sayyidina Rasulullah ﷺ (Salla lahu alayhi wa'ale hi Wasallam) said: 'I do not lean and eat'."

(Kitab'Ash-Shifa)

Sayyidina Aayeshaa Siddiqua (RadiyAllahu Anha) says: "Till the passing of Sayyidina Rasulullah ﷺ (Salla lahu alayhi wa'ale hi Wasallam), their ﷺ family never ate a full stomach of bread made of barley for two consecutive days".

(Ash'aam-il)

Sayyidina Umar ibn Salamah (RadiyAllahu Anhu) said: Sayyidina Rasulullah ﷺ (Salla lahu alayhi wa'ale hi Wasallam) said: 'O young boy, say the name of Allah (SWT) and eat with your right hand, and eat from what is nearest to you'.

(Sahih Bukhari / Sahih Muslim)

It is narrated that a man ate with his left hand in the presence of Sayyidina Rasulullah ﷺ (Salla lahu alayhi wa'ale hi Wasallam). The Messenger ﷺ of Allah said: 'Eat with your right hand'. He replied: 'I cannot'. The Messenger ﷺ of Allah said: 'May you never be able to'. (As nothing was preventing him from doing so but arrogance). That man was never able to raise it to his mouth again.

(Sahih Muslim)

Sayyidina Anas (RadiyAllahu Anhu) reports that: "Sayyidina Rasulullah ﷺ (Salla lahu alayhi wa'ale hi Wasallam) never ate food from a table, nor from small plates, nor was thin bread ever made for Sayyidina Rasulullah ﷺ (Salla lahu alayhi wa'ale hi Wasallam). Sayyidina Yunus (RadiyAllahu Anhu) says; 'I asked Qataadah: 'Then on what did Sayyidina Rasulullah ﷺ (Salla lahu alayhi wa'ale Wasallam) place and eat their ﷺ food'? He replied: 'On this leather cloth'.

(Ash'aam-il)

Sayyidina Salmaa (RadiyAllahu Anha) says that Sayyidina Imaam Hasan, Sayyidina Abdullah ibn Abbas and Sayyidina Abdullah ibn Ja'far Sadiq, (RadiyAllahu Anhumma) came to her and said, "Cook for us the food that Sayyidina Rasulullah ﷺ (Salla lahu alayhi wa'ale hi Wasallam) liked and ate with pleasure". Sayyidina Salmaa (RadiyAllahu Anha) replied, "O' my children, you will not like it now." (It was only liked in times of hardships). They (RadiyAllahu Anhumma) replied, "Yes, we will surely like it". Sayyidina Salmaa (RadiyAllahu Anha) got up and took a bit of barley, (crushed it) and put it in a pot, and poured a little olive oil over it. Then crushed some chillies and spices and added it to the pot and served it, saying, "This is what Sayyidina Rasulullah ﷺ (Salla lahu alayhi wa'ale hi Wasallam) loved (and ate with pleasure)."

(Ash'aam-il)

The Dress of the Messenger ﷺ of Allah

Sayyidina Jundub ibn Makith (RadiyAllahu Anhu) narrates that the Messenger ﷺ of Allah would wear good clothes, when welcoming a delegation, and would order the same for his ﷺ companions to do likewise.' Another hadith relates from the Messenger ﷺ of Allah; 'You are going to visit your brothers, so repair your saddles and make sure that you are dressed well'.

(Harun Yahya)

The blessed dress of Sayyidina Rasulullah ﷺ (Salla lahu alayhi wa'ale hi Wasallam) was simple in nature, as it is disliked that men adorn themselves with fancy clothes, as women do. The garments that are praised are those which are clean, and of moderate quality. The clothes worn must not be to signify pride, or give others the impression of being wealthy or being lavish. The Shariah, does not allow for this.

A few narrations from 'Ash'aam-il Muhammidiyyah ﷺ', the compilation of Ahadith based on the description of Sayyidina Rasulullah ﷺ (Salla lahu alayhi wa'ale hi Wasallam), by Imam Tirmidhi (Rh), can be found below;

The garments worn by Sayyidina Rasulullah ﷺ (Salla lahu alayhi wa'ale hi Wasallam) were coarse, and would consist of a lower sheet, and an outer garment.

(Qadi Iyad)

Sayyidina Ibn Abbaas (RadiyAllahu Anhu) says that Sayyidina Rasulullah ﷺ (Salla lahu alayhi wa'ale hi Wasallam) would say: "Choose white clothing, as it is the best clothing. White clothing should be worn whilst living, and the dead should be buried in white."

(Tirmidhi)

It is reported from Sayyidina Aayeshaa Siddiqua (RadiyAllahu Anha) that: "Sayyidina Rasulullah ﷺ (Salla lahu alayhi wa'ale hi Wasallam) did not leave any of the morning food for the evening, nor any of the evening food for the morning. Sayyidina Rasulullah ﷺ (Salla lahu alayhi wa'ale hi Wasallam) possessed only one each, of a lower garment, long shirt, sheet (body wrap), shoes or any other clothing. Sayyidina Rasulullah ﷺ (Salla lahu alayhi wa'ale hi Wasallam) did not have a pair of any of these".

(Tirmidhi)

Sayyidina Abu Burdah bin Musa Al-Ash'ari (RadiyAllahu Anhu) reports, "Sayyidina Aayeshaa Siddiqua (RadiyAllahu Anha) showed us a patched sheet, and a thick coarse lower garment, then said, "Sayyidina Rasulullah ﷺ (Salla lahu alayhi wa'ale hi Wasallam) passed away wearing these clothes."

(Ash'aam-il)

Sayyidina Qurrah bin Iyaas (RadiyAllahu Anhu) relates: "I came with a group from the tribe of Muzeenah to make bay'ah (give allegiance) to Sayyidina Rasulullah ﷺ (Salla lahu alayhi wa'ale hi Wasallam). The button loop of Sayyidina Rasulullah's ﷺ (Salla lahu alayhi wa'ale hi Wasallam) shirt was open. I put my hand in the collar of Sayyidina Rasulullah's ﷺ (Salla lahu alayhi wa'ale hi

Wasallam) shirt to touch the Seal of Prophethood (to gain barakah)".

(Tirmidhi)

When Sayyidina Qurrah ibn Iyaas (Ra) visited the Messenger ﷺ of Allah, he found the collar of the Messenger's ﷺ shirt open. It is a characteristic of one who loves, that every act of his beloved sinks into his heart. Sayyidina Urwah (RadiyAllahu Anhu), who is a narrator of this hadith says: "I have never seen Mu'aawiyah (bin Qurrah – (RadiyAllahu Anhu)) and his son button up their collars since. Be it summer or winter, their collars were always open". This shows their love for Sayyidina Rasulullah ﷺ (Salla lahu alayhi wa'ale hi Wasallam), as they adopted this *'Sunnah'*, instantly. The Sahaabah (RadiyAllahu Anhumma) did not worry about which of his ﷺ 'Sunnah' are obligatory, and which are recommended. They took everything from the Messenger ﷺ of Allah. They lived the Words of Allah (SWT) in the Noble Qur'an;

'Whatsoever the Messenger gives you, take it. And whatsoever he forbids, abstain from it and keep your duty to Allah'. (Al'Qur'an; 59:7)

Sayyidina Abu Hurayrah (RadiyAllahu Anhu) relates that the blessed sandals of Sayyidina Rasulullah ﷺ (Salla lahu alayhi wa'ale hi Wasallam) had two straps.

(Ash'aam-il)

Sayyidina Jaabir (RadiyAllahu Anhu) says that Sayyidina Rasulullah ﷺ (Salla lahu alayhi wa'ale hi Wasallam) prohibited eating with the left hand, or the wearing of one shoe only.

(Ash'aam-il)

The above narration is legislation of the manner in which we should eat. The Messenger ﷺ of Allah prohibited eating and drinking using the left hand, and the wearing of one shoe. Shoes are made to be worn in pairs.

The Speech of the Messenger ﷺ of Allah

The Messenger ﷺ of Allah, was the greatest of the Arabs in oratory and beauty of speech, and has been narrated to have said, 'I am the greatest orator among the Arabs'.

(Ash-Shifa)

Beauty of speech consists of many factors. These can include; being precise; economical with words; being articulate, possessing accurate grammar; having a varied tone; and pace. These factors indicate if someone possesses eloquence. As discussed earlier, it is debatable whether eloquence of speech is a natural quality or one that can be acquired. Yet there are aspects of the speech of the Messenger ﷺ of Allah, which cannot be present through natural disposition; or be acquired through education. Such perfection of speech, can only have been present through the miraculous nature of his ﷺ attributes.

The hadith previously mentioned, includes the fact that the Messenger ﷺ of Allah was Granted knowledge of all words. In addition to this, the Messenger ﷺ possessed eloquence to such a great degree that people would come to his ﷺ gathering to debate with him ﷺ, and would be mesmerized by his ﷺ speech. The Arabs were great linguists and orators, they were renowned for their poetry; and artistry in debate. Yet even the greatest of them, could not match Sayyidina Rasulullah ﷺ (Salla lahu alayhi wa'ale hi Wasallam) in speech. They were left confounded, and knew this was not the speech of an ordinary man. This eloquence of speech was among the miraculous qualities of the Messenger ﷺ of Allah, and was proof of his ﷺ Prophethood. As Ibn Kathir wrote in *'Qasas ul' Ambiya'*, Allah (SWT) Would Grant Miracles to His Prophets, according to the time in which they came.

Sayyidina Musa (Alayhi Salaam) - *Moses* came in a time when magic was widely used, so Allah (SWT) Granted him the 'Staff' which overcame the magic presented before him. Sayyidina Eesa (Alayhi Salaam) – *Jesus*, was Granted the miracle to cure the sick, and this was in a time when the field of medicine was moving forward rapidly. Sayyidina Rasulullah ﷺ (Salla lahu alayhi wa'ale hi Wasallam), was Granted mastery of language, as has been discussed by Imam Qadi Iyad (Rh). In his renowned book; *'Kitab'Ash-Shifa'*, the great Imam explains that the Messenger ﷺ of Allah knew all the dialects of the different Arab tribes. The Messenger ﷺ of Allah would converse with the different tribes, using their own style of rhetoric, and their own way of communication. This was also crucial when people from different parts of the *Hijaz* (Ancient Arabia), would come to debate, and the Messenger ﷺ of Allah could debate using their style of language, and even the companions (RadiyAllahu Anhumma) would have to enquire later of what was discussed.

Below are examples of the eloquence of the speech of the Messenger ﷺ of Allah.

Sayyidina Aayeshaa Siddiqua (RadiyAllahu Anha) relates that the speech of Sayyidina Rasulullah ﷺ (Salla lahu alayhi wa'ale hi Wasallam) was not quick and continuous as that of yours. Sayyidina Rasulullah ﷺ (Salla lahu alayhi wa'ale hi Wasallam) spoke clearly, word for word. A person sitting in that blessed company remembered what Sayyidina Rasulullah ﷺ (Salla lahu alayhi wa'ale hi Wasallam) said.

(Tirmidhi)

Sayyidina Ayeshaa Siddiqua (RadiyAllahu Anha) has been narrated to have said that the Messenger ﷺ of Allah would say something in such a way that a person could have counted his ﷺ words if he had so wished.

Footprints of the Messenger ﷺ of Allah

(Kitab' Ash-Shifa)

It has been related in the above hadith found in 'Sahih Bukhari' and 'Sahih Muslim' that the blessed words of Sayyidina Rasulullah ﷺ (Salla lahu alayhi wa'ale hi Wasallam) were so concise, they could actually be counted. Below are extracts from a comprehensive hadith, which has been mentioned several times in this work.

Sayyidina Imaam Hasan ibn Ali (RadiyAllahu Anhu) says, "I asked my (maternal) uncle; Hind ibn Abi Haalah, who always described the noble features of Sayyidina Rasulullah ﷺ (Salla lahu alayhi wa'ale hi Wasallam), to describe to me the manner in which Sayyidina Rasulullah ﷺ (Salla lahu alayhi wa'ale hi Wasallam) spoke. He replied that Sayyidina Rasulullah ﷺ (Salla lahu alayhi wa'ale hi Wasallam) was always worried (about the Hereafter). And was always busy thinking (about the Attributes of Allah (SWT) and the betterment of the Ummah). Due to these things, Sayyidina Rasulullah ﷺ (Salla lahu alayhi wa'ale hi Wasallam) was never free from thought and never rested.

Sayyidina Rasulullah ﷺ (Salla lahu alayhi wa'ale hi Wasallam) spoke concisely, where the words are less and meaning more. Every word was clearer than the previous one. There was no nonsensical talk, nor was there half-talks, where the meaning was not complete and could not be grasped.

Sayyidina Rasulullah ﷺ (Salla lahu alayhi wa'ale hi Wasallam) was not short-tempered, and did not disgrace anyone. Sayyidina Rasulullah ﷺ (Salla lahu alayhi wa'ale hi Wasallam) always greatly appreciated the Blessings of Allah (SWT) even though it might be very small, and did not criticize it.

Sayyidina Rasulullah ﷺ (Salla lahu alayhi wa'ale hi Wasallam) did not criticize food, nor over-praised it.

(The reason for not criticizing food is clear, because it is a blessing from Allah (SWT), and the reason for not over-praising it is because that is a sign of indulgence. Nevertheless, Sayyidina Rasulullah ﷺ (Salla lahu alayhi wa'ale hi Wasallam) praised food if it was to make someone happy, and sometimes praised some special things).

Sayyidina Rasulullah ﷺ (Salla lahu alayhi wa'ale hi Wasallam) was never angered for anything materialistic.

(The reason being that Sayyidina Rasulullah ﷺ (Salla lahu alayhi wa'ale hi Wasallam) did not pay much attention and did not care much about material things).

(Ash'aam-il Muhammidiyyah ﷺ)

During the migration – *Hijrah*, the Messenger ﷺ of Allah was accompanied by his ﷺ faithful companion; Sayyidina Abu Bakr Siddique (RadiyAllahu Anhu). As they travelled to Medina, they stopped at a home of a bedouin lady, her name was 'Umm Ma'bad'. She was not aware of who they were, and told them that she did not have anything to offer them. There had been a famine at the time. Even her goats were so mal-nourished, they could not give milk.

However the Messenger ﷺ of Allah, asked for a bowl from her, and preceded to milk the goats. Among the miracles of Sayyidina Rasulullah ﷺ (Salla lahu alayhi wa'ale hi Wasallam), is that his ﷺ blessed touch made things abundant. The Messenger ﷺ of Allah began to milk the goats, and they began giving milk. The milk they produced was so great, that all the utensils in the house of Umm Ma'bad were filled, yet the goats remained full.

Later that evening, after the Messenger ﷺ of Allah departed, Umm Ma'bad's husband returned home. She tried to explain about where this abundant milk had come from, and about their blessed guests. In books of Ahadith, the words she used to describe the Messenger ﷺ of Allah are mentioned. Umm Ma'bad (RadiyAllahu Anha), explained that this man was beautiful from afar, and was even more beautiful from near.

She described the Messenger ﷺ of Allah as a 'blessed man'. She explained the speech of Sayyidina Rasulullah ﷺ (Salla lahu alayhi wa'ale hi Wasallam) as being 'sweet, distinct, without using too few or too many words'. Umm Ma'bad (Ra) described the words of the Messenger ﷺ of Allah as being *'like they were threaded pearls'*.

(Ash-Shifa)

The Intellect of the Messenger ﷺ of Allah

The intellect and sound understanding of Sayyidina Rasulullah ﷺ (Salla lahu alayhi wa'ale hi Wasallam), was not a result of formal education, or enhanced through sitting in learned circles. The intellect and acuteness of the understanding of the Messenger ﷺ of Allah, was through Divine Inspiration. Every physical attribute of the Messenger ﷺ of Allah, are among his ﷺ miracles, and have been explained as such in books of *Seerah*.

In the work of Imam Qadi Iyad (Rh), he has included a reference from Wahb ibn Munabbih; *'I have read seventy one books, and in all of them I have found that the Messenger ﷺ of Allah had the most superior intellect, and best opinion'*.

Ibn Munabbih has concluded that all the intelligence given to the creation from beginning to the end, is like a grain of sand in comparison to the Messenger ﷺ of Allah. This is the reason why the judgment of the Messenger ﷺ of Allah has to be accepted in all matters, and constitutes as the Judgement of Allah (SWT). This ruling is found in the Noble Qur'an;

'But no, by your Lord, they can have no real faith until they make you judge in all disputes between them, and find in their-selves no resistance against your decisions, and submit with the fullest submission'. (Al Qur'an: 4:65).

According to sound traditions, the Messenger ﷺ of Allah had knowledge of all matters, and was aware of what was happening even when a matter took place behind him ﷺ. It has been narrated that

Sayyidina Rasulullah ﷺ (Salla lahu alayhi wa'ale hi Wasallam) corrected the prayer of the companions (RadiyAllahu Anhumma), even though they were praying behind him ﷺ in congregation.

(Al Muwatta)

The Courage of the Messenger ﷺ of Allah

In books of Seerah, very rarely are narrations included in regards to the courage of Sayyidina Rasulullah ﷺ (Salla lahu alayhi wa'ale hi Wasallam). The mercy, generosity, compassion, patience, forbearance, are always included, but the courage of the Messenger ﷺ of Allah is rarely mentioned in detail. Among the Companions (RadiyAllahu Anhumma), it was known that the most difficult task was for that companion (Ra) who was appointed to guard the Messenger ﷺ of Allah, during battle. This was because the Messenger ﷺ of Allah would always be in the front line, closest to the enemy. This responsibility was given to Sayyidina Abu Bakr Siddique (RadiyAllahu Anhu), until Allah (SWT) Revealed the verse that the Messenger ﷺ of Allah has been protected from people;

'Allah Will Protect you from the people'. **(Al Qur'an; 5:67)**

Sayyidina Ibn Umar (RadiyAllahu Anhu) said, 'I never saw anyone more courageous, generous, or pleasing than the Messenger ﷺ of Allah'.

(Ad-Darimi).

Even during the battle of Hunayn, when the believers were ambushed, and it momentarily caused disarray among the Muslim army, it was the Messenger ﷺ of Allah who remained firm, and advanced towards the enemy. It has been narrated that at this time, only Sayyidina Abu Sufyan (Ra) was with him ﷺ, holding back the reins of his ﷺ horse.

(Ash-Shifa)

Sayyidina Ali ibn Abi Talib (RadiyAllahu Anhu) narrates, 'When the situation was intense, and the fighting was fierce, we took

protection by the Messenger ﷺ of Allah, none was closer to the enemy than him ﷺ. I saw the Messenger ﷺ of Allah on the day of Badr, we were close to him ﷺ, and none was closer to the enemy than him ﷺ. The Messenger ﷺ of Allah, was the bravest person on that day'.

(An-Nasai)

One night, in Medina t'ul Munnawarah, there was a disturbance, and as the Companions, May Allah (SWT) Be Pleased with them, set off to find out what was happening, they met the Messenger ﷺ of Allah, who was already returning, having found the source of the alarm. A horse belonging to Abu Talha (Ra) had got loose. The sword was hanging by his ﷺ side, and the Messenger ﷺ of Allah told the companions (RadiyAllahu Anhum) not to be concerned.

(Shaam'il Habib al Mustafa ﷺ)

The Strength of the Messenger ﷺ of Allah

The physical prowess of a man, is one of his qualities, and a means of honour. This is why the strength of the Messenger ﷺ of Allah was greater than the rest of creation. The Arabs were considered to be the strongest of all, and among them, it was the tribe of Quraysh who were renowned for their might. The Messenger ﷺ of Allah was the strongest among them.

There was a famous wrestler in the Arab lands, by the name of 'Rukana'. He challenged the Messenger ﷺ of Allah in a contest. Sayyidina Rasulullah ﷺ (Salla lahu alayhi wa'ale hi Wasallam) asked him what the prize will be for the winner. Rukana replied, 'Sheep will be given to the winner from the loser'. The Messenger ﷺ of Allah threw down Rukana at once, and pinned him down. Rukana couldn't believe what had happened to him, and asked for another match. Once again, the Messenger ﷺ of Allah defeated him, and once again, Rukana asked for another contest. In total, the Messenger ﷺ of Allah pinned Rukana down three times. Rukana accepted Islam, after experiencing the tremendous strength of the Messenger ﷺ of Allah. The Messenger ﷺ of Allah, returned the sheep back to him.

(Sham'ail al-Habib al-Mustafa ﷺ)

A similar incident has been narrated about another great wrestler; 'Abul Aswad Jami'. He was so strong that he would pin a cow to the ground, and ten strong men would try to pull it from under him, but would not be able to. He challenged Sayyidina Rasulullah ﷺ (Salla lahu alayhi wa'ale hi Wasallam) and promised he would embrace Islam if defeated. Abul Jami was also defeated by the Messenger ﷺ of Allah, but failed to accept Islam.

(Al Mawahib)

During the digging of the trench, before the famous battle; 'Battle of the Trench', in which the believers repelled an attack on Medina t'ul Munnawarah, by digging a large trench around the city. This was Sayyidina Salman Farsi's (RadiyAllahu Anhu) idea. The companions (RadiyAllahu Anhumma) came across a large rock, which they could not break. Even the strength of Sayyidina Ali ibn Abi Talib, and Sayyidina Umar Ibn Khattab, May Allah (SWT) Be Pleased with them, could not move this rock. The blessed companions called upon Sayyidina Rasulullah ﷺ (Salla lahu alayhi wa'ale hi Wasallam). The Messenger ﷺ of Allah struck the rock once, and it shattered. The companions (Ra) also noticed that there were small rocks tied around the blessed waist of the Messenger ﷺ of Allah, due to having not eaten for three days.

(Al Burhan Sharif)

It is included in narrations, during an Umrah, when the Messenger ﷺ of Allah was accompanied by one hundred pilgrims, for the pilgrimage to Makka. The Messenger ﷺ of Allah slaughtered sixty-three camels with his ﷺ own blessed hand, and Sayyidina Ali ibn Talib (Ra) did the rest. The slaughtered animals were then cooked together in the same pot. It is the blessed Sunnah, to eat from what has been slaughtered by your own hand.

(Shama'il Habib al-Mustafa ﷺ)

PART III – The PROPHETIC CHARACTER

Introduction

The one who possesses power, can never be just. This has proven to be the case for so many leaders and kings, who succumb to the known pitfalls of having complete authority. However Sayyidina Rasulullah ﷺ (Salla lahu alayhi wa'ale hi Wasallam) remained steadfast in every state, whether that of a modest dweller, or that of a supreme ruler. The character of Sayyidina Rasulullah ﷺ (Salla lahu alayhi wa'ale hi Wasallam), was conclusive proof of his ﷺ truthfulness, and thus of his ﷺ Message. Even the leaders of Makka who turned against the Messenger ﷺ of Allah, would swear on his ﷺ truthfulness, and behind closed doors professed that Sayyidina Muhammad ﷺ is a truthful man. To forgive when you possess the might to punish, is the sign of having mercy, and this is the quality that the Messenger ﷺ of Allah possessed, and the reason people embraced Islam. Sayyidina Rasulullah ﷺ (Salla lahu alayhi wa'ale hi Wasallam), sat with the poor of his ﷺ community, and listened to them, and granted rights to the oppressed, bringing a revolution of the like not witnessed before in the Arab peninsula. Sayyidina Rasulullah ﷺ (Salla lahu alayhi wa'ale hi Wasallam) fulfilled the rights of his ﷺ family, and his ﷺ neighbour alike, and even as a Statesman, remained moderate and just in all affairs. The legacy of Sayyidina Rasulullah ﷺ (Salla lahu alayhi wa'ale hi Wasallam) cannot be measured, as his ﷺ character and achievements came from the Divine Will of Allah (SWT), but it is reflected through his faithful companions (RadiyAllahu Anhumma). The men who change history, behind whose footprints the world walk forever, are those who leave behind men who reflect their teachings, and character. Sayyidina Rasulullah ﷺ (Salla lahu alayhi wa'ale hi Wasallam) left behind men of valour like; Sayyidina Ali ibn Abi Talib; men of truth like Sayyidina Abu Bakr Siddique; men of fortitude like Sayyidina Umar Ibn Khattab, and men of modesty like Sayyidina Uthman Ibn Affan. May Allah (SWT) Be Pleased with them.

And Verily, you (O Muhammad ﷺ) are on an exalted standard of character.

(Al' Qur'an; 68:4)

In the Noble Qur'an, the Final Word of Allah (SWT) which cannot be altered even by a single letter, and remains as it is until the End of time, includes references to the esteemed character of the Messenger ﷺ of Allah. This is why Allah (SWT) Has Stated in over forty places in His Noble Book that obedience to His Final Messenger ﷺ, is obedience to His Own Commands. These two commands remain connected, just as the blessed name of the Messenger ﷺ of Allah, follows that of Allah (SWT).
Allah (SWT) Revealed the blessed character of Sayyidina Rasulullah ﷺ (Salla lahu alayhi wa'ale hi Wasallam) as being one of His Signs, and therefore they have been revealed in His Ultimate Book of Guidance.

The character of the Messenger ﷺ of Allah was also revealed to the previous nations, in their Books. It has been narrated by Sayyidina Ata' ibn Yasar, who said, 'I met Abdullah ibn Amr ibn al-Aas, and asked him to describe the Messenger ﷺ of Allah. He replied, 'Certainly. By Allah, some of the characteristics by which the Messenger ﷺ of Allah is described in the Qur'an, are also found in the Torah. It says, 'O' Prophet ﷺ, We have sent you as a witness, a bringer of good news; and a warner; and a refuge for the unlettered. You are my slave, and my Messenger. I have called you the one on whom people rely, one who is neither coarse, nor vulgar, and who does not shout in the market-place, nor repays evil with evil, but rather pardons and forgives....'. Through another narration, by Sayyidina Ibn Ishaq (Ra), mentions, 'Who does not shout in the market place, nor uses obscene language, nor indecent words. I open him ﷺ to every excellent quality, and I give him ﷺ every noble trait'. These references are found in Imam Qadi Iyad's work; *'Kitab'Ash-Shifa'*.

The blessed wife of the Messenger ﷺ of Allah, has been narrated to have said, 'The character of the Messenger ﷺ of Allah, was the Qur'an. The Messenger ﷺ of Allah was pleased by what it states as pleasing, and angry according to what it states as hateful'.

(Al Bayhaqi)

This narration has been recorded as the response to when people would ask Sayyidina Ayeshaa Siddiqua (RadiyAllahu Anha) about the character of the Messenger ﷺ of Allah. The response Sayyidina Aayeshaa Siddiqua (Ra), would give was that whatever was found in the Noble Qur'an, whatever it orders, was the character of the Messenger ﷺ of Allah. The *tafsir*, which is the interpretation and elaboration of the Noble Qur'an, is everything you find in the Messenger ﷺ of Allah.

The Mercy of the Messenger ﷺ of Allah

Among the qualities that Allah (SWT) describes of the Messenger ﷺ of Allah, in the Noble Qur'an, is that of being 'Merciful'. In fact the greatest honour that Allah (SWT) Can Bestow upon His Creation, is to adorn them with His Own Attributes. AL Husayn ibn al-Fadl, said, 'He Honoured His Messenger ﷺ with two of His Own attributes, the 'compassionate'; and the 'merciful'; *'ra'uf*; and *'rahim'*. (Ash-Shifa)

Allah (SWT) Says in the Noble Qur'an;

'Allah was Kind to the believers when He sent to them a Messenger from among themselves'. (Al' Qur'an; 3:164)

Allah (SWT) Has Revealed in another verse;

'We did not send you except as a mercy to the worlds'. (Al' Qur'an; 21:107)

The above verse has been the subject of extensive commentary, as how Allah (SWT) Used certain words to describe that the Messenger ﷺ of Allah, as being sent as a *'Mercy to the Worlds'*. Sayyidina Abu Bakr Muhammad ibn Tahir (Rh), has discussed that, 'Allah (SWT) Imbued the Messenger ﷺ with Mercy, so that his ﷺ very existence was mercy, and all his ﷺ sublime qualities and attributes were mercy to all creatures'. (Ash-Shifa)

The specific language used in this verse, is that **'We did not send you except as a mercy to the worlds'**. This verse can only be understood, as being that the absolute reason for sending the Messenger ﷺ of Allah is to be a 'mercy', except which there is no other reason. The essence of this verse cannot be diluted as it contains the absolute statement that the

Messenger ﷺ of Allah is a 'mercy to the worlds', except which nothing else can be implied. Sayyidina Rasulullah ﷺ (Salla lahu alayhi wa'ale hi Wasallam) was a 'mercy' for the entire creation; mankind; jinn; animals, as numerous narrations prove. It has been reported from Sayyidina Ibn Abbas (Ra), who explained that the, 'Messenger ﷺ of Allah was a mercy for the believers by purifying them, or guiding them. A mercy for the non-believers, as the Messenger ﷺ being amongst them, deferred their punishment, and for the hypocrites, as the Messenger ﷺ prevented them from being killed'. (Ash-Shifa)

Allah (SWT) Mentions in His Noble Qur'an, *'It was by a mercy from Allah that you were kind to them, if you had been harsh, they would have fled'.* **(3:159)**

This verse has been explained by As-Samarqandi, as meaning, 'Allah (SWT) Reminding the believers that the Messenger ﷺ is merciful, compassionate and lenient towards them'. This was a favour onto the believers, as they always found the Messenger ﷺ of Allah, magnanimous, kind and gentle.

(Qadi Iyad)

Allah (SWT) Would console His beloved Messenger ﷺ when the people of Makka would reject his ﷺ message. This aggrieved the Messenger ﷺ of Allah, as the Messenger ﷺ wished for everyone to be saved from the hell-fire. In the Noble Qur'an, this verse was revealed;

'We know that what they say grieves you. It is not you they reject, but the evil-doers, it is the Signs of Allah they deny'. **(6:33)**

Imam Qadi Iyad (Rh) explains that Allah (SWT) comforted the Messenger ﷺ of Allah, with these beautiful words, showing that his ﷺ esteemed place is secure whether the non-believers accept the Message or not. Sayyidina Jibrail (As) told the Messenger ﷺ of Allah, 'They know you tell the truth'. The people of Makka would call the

Messenger ﷺ, 'trustworthy', and 'truthful', long before they were aware of his ﷺ Prophethood.

Further narrations discussing the mercy of Sayyidina Rasulullah ﷺ (Salla lahu alayhi wa'ale hi Wasallam), are included below;

Sayyidina Anas bin Maalik (RadiyAllahu Anhu) says: "I remained in the service of Sayyidina Rasulullah ﷺ (Salla lahu alayhi wa'ale hi Wasallam) for ten years. Sayyidina Rasulullah ﷺ (Salla lahu alayhi wa'ale hi Wasallam) never once said 'Uff' to me. When I did something, Sayyidina Rasulullah ﷺ (Salla lahu alayhi wa'ale hi Wasallam) never asked me; 'why did you do this? When I did not do a certain task, Sayyidina Rasulullah ﷺ (Salla lahu alayhi wa'ale hi Wasallam) never asked me that why I did not do it. Sayyidina Rasulullah ﷺ (Salla lahu alayhi wa'ale hi Wasallam) had the best character among all people (and also possessed the most excellent features, so much so,) that I never felt a silk cloth, nor pure silk, nor any other thing softer than the blessed palm of Sayyidina Rasulullah ﷺ (Salla lahu alayhi wa'ale hi Wasallam). Nor did I smell any musk or any other fragrance, more sweet smelling than the sweat of Sayyidina Rasulullah ﷺ (Salla lahu alayhi wa'ale hi Wasallam)".

(Tirmidhi)

Sayyidina Aayeshaa Siddiqua (RadiyAllahu Anha) reports, that: "It was not the blessed nature of Sayyidina Rasulullah ﷺ (Salla lahu alayhi wa'ale hi Wasallam) to talk indecently and did not engage himself ﷺ in the use of obscene language. Nor did Sayyidina Rasulullah ﷺ (Salla lahu alayhi wa'ale hi Wasallam) shout and talk

in the marketplace (which is against dignity). Sayyidina Rasulullah ﷺ (Salla lahu alayhi wa'ale hi Wasallam) did not avenge a bad deed with a bad one, but forgave it, and thereafter did not even mention it".

(Tirmidhi)

Sayyidina Aayeshaa Siddiqua (RadiyAllahu Anha) reports: "Sayyidina Rasulullah ﷺ (Salla lahu alayhi wa'ale hi Wasallam) did not hit anything with his ﷺ blessed hands, besides the time when Sayyidina Rasulullah ﷺ (Salla lahu alayhi wa'ale hi Wasallam) made *jihaad* (Struggle / fought) in the Path of Allah (SWT). Sayyidina Rasulullah ﷺ (Salla lahu alayhi wa'ale hi Wasallam) did not hit a servant nor a woman (wife, slave girl etc.)".

(Ash'aam-il)

When the Messenger ﷺ of Allah, visited the land of Taif, and was subjected to the worst treatment at the hands of its residents. The people of Taif rejected the Messenger ﷺ of Allah, and began to throw stones that injured the Messenger ﷺ of Allah. Upon leaving Taif, his ﷺ blood flowed down his ﷺ blessed body and reached his ﷺ ankles. Angel Jibrail (As) was sent by Allah (SWT) to console the Messenger ﷺ of Allah, and said, 'Allah (SWT) Has Ordered the angels of the mountains to obey whatever you tell them to do'. The angel of the mountains greeted the Messenger ﷺ of Allah, and said, 'I will crush these people between the two mountains of Makka, if you so wish'. The Messenger ﷺ of Allah did not wish this for even those who injured, and tormented him through their streets. The Messenger ﷺ replied, 'I hope that Allah will bring forth from their loins those who will worship Allah Alone, and not associate anything with Him'.

(Sahih Bukhari & Sahih Muslim)

During the Battle of Uhud, the Messenger ﷺ of Allah was severely injured, and suffered lacerations to his ﷺ blessed face, and had a tooth shattered. This was unbearable for his ﷺ Companions (Ra) who asked the Messenger ﷺ of Allah to curse the non-believers. The Messenger ﷺ of Allah responded that, 'I was not sent to curse, but I was sent as a summoner, and as a mercy. Ya' Allah, Guide my people, for they do not know'.

(Qadi Iyad)

There are extensive references in books of Ahadith, and in the accounts of Seerah that the Messenger ﷺ of Allah continued to forgive those who inflicted torment on him ﷺ. This mercy was the most significant factor in turning his ﷺ enemies to Islam. Allamah Muhammad Iqbal (Rh) expressed this beautifully; *'The Messenger ﷺ of Allah was merciful, when people could not even be just, the Messenger ﷺ was content, when people could not even be patient'.*

The Messenger ﷺ of Allah forgave the Jewish woman who put poison in the sheep and served this to him ﷺ, and later confessed.

(Tirmidhi)

Ghawrath ibn al-Harith, had made plans to assassinate Sayyidina Rasulullah ﷺ (Salla lahu alayhi wa'ale hi Wasallam), and found him ﷺ alone, sitting under a tree. Ghawrath ibn al-Harith had his sword with him, and said to the Messenger ﷺ of Allah, 'Who will save you from me today'? The Messenger ﷺ replied, 'Allah'. At that point, the sword fell out of ibn al-Harith's hand, and the Messenger ﷺ of Allah picked it up, and asked, 'Who will protect you from me, now'? Ibn al-Harith replied, 'Punish me in the best manner'. The Messenger ﷺ of Allah pardoned him. When

Ghawrath ibn al-Harith returned to his people, he said, 'I have come to you from the best of people'.

(Sahih Bukhari & Sahih Muslim)

Many books of Ahadith mention one particular incident which is viewed as the worst treatment of the people of Quraysh towards the Messenger ﷺ of Allah. Sayyidina Rasulullah ﷺ (Salla lahu alayhi wa'ale hi Wasallam) was praying in the enclosure surrounding the Kaaba. Uqba ibn Abu Mu'ayt, drew his rope around the blessed neck of the Messenger ﷺ of Allah, and began choking him ﷺ. At this time, Sayyidina Abu Bakr Siddique (RadiyAllahu Anhu) approached and pulled the man off, he wept and said, 'Shame on you, would you murder a man for saying 'Allah Ho Akbar'.

(Ibn Kathir)

It has been reported by Sayyidina Ibn Masud (Ra), 'The Messenger ﷺ of Allah was careful when admonishing us, fearing that it would tire us'.

(Sahih Bukhari)

Sayyidina Rasulullah ﷺ (Salla lahu alayhi wa'ale hi Wasallam) would always choose the easier of two paths for his ﷺ companions, as long as it did not involve transgressing the laws of the Shariah. An example of this is that the Messenger ﷺ of Allah forbade the companions (Ra) to spend the entire night in worship and neglect their families. Fasting of 'Al-Wisal', which is continuous fasting for more than one day, was not permitted for the Sahaabah, May Allah (SWT) Be Pleased with them. It has also been mentioned in traditions that the Messenger ﷺ of Allah would shorten the congregational prayer upon hearing cries of the children in the homes of Medina, so that their mothers could return to them.

(Ash-Shifa)

The Messenger ﷺ of Allah, said, (It happens that) 'I start the prayer intending to prolong it, but on hearing the cries of a child, I shorten the prayer because I know that the cries of the child will incite its mother's passions.'

(Sahih Bukhari)

In the collection of miracles related to the Messenger ﷺ of Allah, it has been mentioned that a slave-girl asked the Messenger ﷺ of Allah for food, while the Messenger ﷺ was eating. The Messenger ﷺ of Allah gave her food that was in front of him ﷺ, but she asked boldly for the food in his ﷺ blessed mouth. The Messenger ﷺ of Allah gave her what was in his ﷺ blessed mouth. Once she had consumed it, she was overtaken by modesty. So much that she was regarded as among the most modest women in Medina t'ul Munnawarah.

(At-Tabarani)

This above narration is also an example of the miracle of whatever is touched by the Messenger ﷺ of Allah, becomes a cure and blessing. But it also shows his ﷺ mercy, as the Messenger ﷺ never refused anyone. SubhanAllah Ya Rasulullah ﷺ.

The Generosity of the Messenger ﷺ of Allah

Generosity can be evident in many ways, which does not only include being generous with giving charity, or by assisting the poor. One can also be generous with their time, and with their advice. This is especially rare with people who are famous.

Among the great characteristics of Sayyidina Rasulullah ﷺ (Salla lahu alayhi wa'ale hi Wasallam) was to be generous in all regard, which included assisting the needy; being kind to adults, and gentle to children. Sayyidina Rasulullah ﷺ (Salla lahu alayhi wa'ale hi Wasallam) was always gracious, and humble, which ensured that anyone could approach him ﷺ, and present their needs. This quality is among the rarest, especially with people who are highly-regarded. There are narrations in this regard below;

The Messenger ﷺ of Allah would shake hands and would not withdraw his ﷺ hand till the other man withdrew his.

(Tirmidhi)

When Sayyidina Rasulullah ﷺ (Salla lahu alayhi wa'ale hi Wasallam) addressed a person, it would be by turning his ﷺ whole blessed body towards that person.

(Tirmidhi)

Sayyidina Rasulullah ﷺ (Salla lahu alayhi wa'ale hi Wasallam) was never seen to put forward his ﷺ blessed knees in front of one who was sitting before him ﷺ, which would restrict their space.

(Ash'aam-il)

The Messenger ﷺ of Allah would call his ﷺ Companions, May Allah (SWT) Be Pleased with them, by their *'Kunya'*, family name, with honour, and would give them a 'Kunya' if they did not have one.

(Ash-Shifa)

Sayyidina Ibn Abbaas (RadiyAllahu Anhu) says: "Sayyidina Rasulullah ﷺ (Salla lahu alayhi wa'ale hi Wasallam) was the most generous among people in performing good deeds (No one could compare with Sayyidina Rasulullah ﷺ (Salla lahu alayhi wa'ale hi Wasallam) in generosity.

(Ash-Shifa)

Sayyidina Rasulullah ﷺ (Salla lahu alayhi wa'ale hi Wasallam) led a simple life himself ﷺ, but in giving would exceed a king. At a time of great need, a woman presented him ﷺ with a sheet, and Sayyidina Rasulullah ﷺ (Salla lahu alayhi wa'ale hi Wasallam) wore it due to being in need of it. Then a person came and asked for it, Sayyidina Rasulullah ﷺ (Salla lahu alayhi wa'ale hi Wasallam) presented the sheet to that person. Taking of loans and fulfilling the needs of others, when the creditors came, and if something had come from somewhere, Sayyidina Rasulullah ﷺ (Salla lahu alayhi wa'ale hi Wasallam) would pay the debts, and did not go home till everything was given to the needy.

In the month of Ramadan, Sayyidina Rasulullah ﷺ (Salla lahu alayhi wa'ale hi Wasallam) would be even more generous. In this month when Angel Jibra-eel (Alayhis Salaam) came and recited the Noble Qur'an to Sayyidina Rasulullah ﷺ (Salla lahu alayhi wa'ale hi Wasallam), at that time his ﷺ generosity exceeded the wind that brings forth heavy rains.

(Ash'aam-il)

Sayyidina Rubayyi' bint Mu'awwidh bin 'Af-raa (RadiyAllahu Anha) says: "I brought to Sayyidina Rasulullah ﷺ (Salla lahu alayhi wa'ale hi Wasallam) a tray full of dates, and some small cucumbers. Sayyidina Rasulullah ﷺ (Salla lahu alayhi wa'ale hi Wasallam) gave me a handful of jewellery".

(Tirmidhi)

Sayyidina Jabir Ibn Abdullah (RadiyAllahu Anhu) said, 'The Messenger ﷺ of Allah, was not asked for anything to which the Messenger ﷺ said, 'No''.

(Sahih Bukhari)

The Messenger ﷺ of Allah would give away everything in his ﷺ possession, and if it was not in his ﷺ possession, the Messenger ﷺ would instruct the needy person to borrow what he needed, and the Messenger ﷺ of Allah would repay that debt.

It has been reported by Sayyidina Anas (RadiyAllahu Anhu), 'A man asked the Messenger ﷺ of Allah for something, and the

Messenger ﷺ of Allah gave him all the sheep between two mountains. The man returned to his people and told them that, 'The Messenger ﷺ gives the gift of someone who does not fear poverty'.

(Sahih Muslim)

Sayyidina Rasulullah ﷺ (Salla lahu alayhi wa'ale hi Wasallam) was generous in his ﷺ conduct with others. The companions (RadiyAllahu Anhumma) would say that every person who came in his ﷺ presence would feel as though he was the most beloved person in the eyes of the Messenger ﷺ of Allah.

The Messenger ﷺ of Allah was known for maintaining ties of kinship, and valuing relations and friendships. His ﷺ milk-sister; ash-Shayma, was brought among the captives of Hawazin, and made herself known. The Messenger ﷺ of Allah treated her like a guest, and spread out his ﷺ cloak' for her.

(Al Bayhaqi)

The Messenger ﷺ of Allah would send gifts for the friends of his ﷺ late wife; Sayyidina Khadijah t'ul Kubraa (RadiyAllahu Anha), this has been related by Sayyidina Ayeshaa Siddiqua (RadiyAllahu Anha).

(Sahih Bukhari)

The generosity of Sayyidina Rasulullah ﷺ (Salla lahu alayhi wa'ale hi Wasallam) extended to the young children. The traditions mention how the Messenger ﷺ of Allah extended his ﷺ sujud – prostration, when his ﷺ blessed grandson; Sayyidina Imam

Hussain ibn Ali (RadiyAllahu Anhu) was a child, and climbed on his ﷺ blessed back.

(Sahih Bukhari)

The Messenger ﷺ of Allah would carry his ﷺ blessed granddaughter, Sayyidina Umama bint Zaynab (RadiyAllahu Anha), on his ﷺ blessed shoulders, and even performed the prayer, while holding her in *qiyaam*- standing position, and putting her down in *sujud* - prostration.

(Ash-Shifa)

It has been narrated by Sayyidina Abu'l Abbas al-Mubarrad (RadiyAllahu Anhu) that the Messenger ﷺ of Allah divided his ﷺ time into three parts; one part for his ﷺ Worship; the second part for his ﷺ family; the third for himself ﷺ. His ﷺ own part would be devoted mostly to the people.

(Ash-Shifa)

Sayyidina Anas ibn Malik (Ra) narrated, 'The servants of Medina would bring their vessels of water to the Messenger ﷺ of Allah, in early morning. The Messenger ﷺ would dip his ﷺ blessed fingers into the vessels, even in the cold mornings. They sought blessings through this'.

(Sahih Muslim)

The Modesty of the Messenger ﷺ of Allah

The modesty of a person, is to protect themselves from what would bring shame. Modesty is part of humility, and is connected with protecting your gaze, and being mindful of guarding your chastity. It is perhaps this quality, which people lose most easily.

Allah (SWT) Mentions the need for believers, men and women, to guard their modesty;

'Tell the believing men to lower their gaze and be modest. That is purer for them. Lo! Allah is aware of what they do.

And tell the believing women to lower their gaze and be modest, and to display of their adornment only that which is apparent ….'

(Al' Qur'an; 24: 30-31)

There is no doubt that as with every praiseworthy quality, Sayyidina Rasulullah ﷺ (Salla lahu alayhi wa'ale hi Wasallam) possessed modesty in greater amount than anyone else in the entire creation. Since the birth of the Messenger ﷺ of Allah, no-one had ever seen the Messenger ﷺ unclothed, and this was another of the miracles granted to him ﷺ. Narrations in this regard, are included below;

Sayyidina Abu Sa'eed <u>Kh</u>udari (RadiyAllahu Anhu) says that Sayyidina Rasulullah ﷺ (Salla lahu alayhi wa'ale hi Wasallam) was more modest than a virgin girl in her veil. When Sayyidina Rasulullah ﷺ (Salla lahu alayhi wa'ale hi Wasallam) did not like something, it could be seen on his ﷺ blessed face.

(Ash'aam-il Muhammidiyyah ﷺ)

This narration means that the Messenger ﷺ of Allah was more modest than an unmarried girl, who keeps her veil. In Islamic culture, girls who were unmarried would tend to remain in their rooms, due to their shyness and modesty. In terms of the second part of this narration, it is mentioned that due to excessive modesty, Sayyidina Rasulullah ﷺ (Salla lahu alayhi wa'ale hi Wasallam) would not mention something offensive but it would become apparent in his ﷺ blessed face.

Sayyidina Aayeshaa Siddiqua (RadiyAllahu Anha), the blessed wife of the Messenger ﷺ of Allah, has narrated, 'The Messenger ﷺ of Allah was not lewd, and did not use bad language. The Messenger ﷺ did not shout in the marketplace and did not repay a bad deed with the like. The Messenger ﷺ of Allah would forgive, and overlook'.

(Sahih Bukhari)

These qualities have also been mentioned in the Torah, and have been included in one of the earlier sections.

Sayyidina Aayeshaa Siddiqua (RadiyAllahu Anha), who is *'Umm-e-Mumineen'*, the 'Mother of the believers', as she is one of the wives of the Messenger ﷺ of Allah, would have been the most intimate with the Messenger ﷺ of Allah. However, she mentions in a narration, 'I never saw the Messenger ﷺ of Allah, in a state of undress'.

(Al Bayhaqi)

According to narrations by Sayyidina Ibn Umar (Ra) and others, the Messenger ﷺ of Allah was born circumcised and with his ﷺ umbilical cord already cut. Sayyidina Anas (Ra) related that the

Messenger ﷺ of Allah, said, "One of the signs of the honour that I have been given by my Lord is that I was born circumcised, and no one saw me in a state of undress."

(Al Mawahib)

The Patience of the Messenger ﷺ of Allah

The greatest test for the Prophets of Allah, Peace be upon them, is that of their patience (Sabr), and their forbearance (Hilm). The Prophets of Allah were sent solely to guide mankind, and therefore faced the greatest of trials and tribulations at the hands of their own family, contemporaries and people. The Prophets (As) of Allah were boycotted; ostracized; tormented; slandered, by the nations for whom they came as a guidance. This quality of patience is among the signs of Prophethood. When we face trials in our life, and bear them with patience, we are following a *'Sunnah'*, of the Prophets of Allah. (Alayhimus Salaam)

Sayyidina Rasulullah ﷺ (Salla lahu alayhi wa'ale hi Wasallam) was tested by the people of Makka, they laid thorns on his ﷺ path, waiting for him ﷺ to approach bare-foot. The Messenger ﷺ of Allah was attacked during his ﷺ prayer, and was accused of not being sane, of performing magic, and being rebellious. The Messenger ﷺ of Allah was boycotted by the affluent leaders of Makka, and his ﷺ companions (RadiyAllahu Anhumma) were attacked, and were martyred as they followed his ﷺ message. Yet the Prophet ﷺ overcame those who caused him ﷺ grief, and did not at any time, curse them, or call upon Allah's (SWT) punishment upon them. This is the patience which melted even the hard-hearted, to accept Islam, and these are the signs of the Final Messenger ﷺ, which were foretold in previous scriptures. Narrations in this regard, are included below;

Sayyidina Ayeshaa Siddiqua (RadiyAllahu Anha) has narrated, 'The Messenger ﷺ of Allah, did not take revenge for himself ﷺ, not unless one of Allah's (SWT) Orders was transgressed'.

(Sahih Bukhari / Sahih Muslim / Sunan Abu Daawud)

This is among the sanctuary of rulings, as transgression of the laws of Allah (SWT) cannot be pardoned. However this narration, and many others, show that the Messenger ﷺ of Allah would never seek revenge for harm done to him ﷺ.

Sayyidina Zayd Ibn Sa'nah (RadiyAllahu Anhu) who was once a Jew, related: "There was not a sign of Prophethood which I did not find in Sayyidina Rasulullah ﷺ (Salla lahu alayhi wa'ale hi Wasallam), however I did not have the opportunity to test two signs. The first is that his ﷺ hilm (gentleness) will overcome his ﷺ anger. The second is, the more one acts foolishly towards him ﷺ, his ﷺ tolerance will increase. I looked for a chance to test these two signs, and kept on coming and going to his ﷺ gatherings.

One day, Sayyidina Rasulullah ﷺ (Salla lahu alayhi wa'ale hi Wasallam) came out of his ﷺ house and Sayyidina Ali ibn Abi Talib (RadiyAllahu Anhu) was with him ﷺ. Just then a badawi type of person came and said: 'O' Rasulullah ﷺ, my community have accepted Islam, and I had told them that if they became Muslims, they shall receive abundant sustenance. However now such a time has come where drought has befallen us. I fear that they will leave Islam. If the idea is suitable, it is suggested that you assist them'. Sayyidina Rasulullah ﷺ (Salla lahu alayhi wa'ale hi Wasallam) looked towards a person who may have been Sayyidina Ali (RadiyAllahu Anhu). He replied, 'Ya Rasulullah ﷺ, there is nothing available'. I was of the Jewish faith at that time, I witnessed this incident, and said. 'O Muhammad ﷺ, if you can do this, a certain amount of dates of a certain person's palm grove be given to me at a fixed time, then I shall pay now in advance and collect the dates at the appointed time'. Sayyidina Rasulullah ﷺ (Salla lahu alayhi wa'ale hi Wasallam) replied that this was possible, and added 'But if you do not stipulate the palm grove, I can make an agreement'. I accepted it, and paid eighty mi<u>th</u>-qaal of gold (according to well-known sayings one mi<u>th</u>-qaal equals 100 grains or four and half maa-shaas approx. four and half grams).

Sayyidina Rasulullah ﷺ (Salla lahu alayhi wa'ale hi Wasallam) gave the gold to this badawi and said to him; 'do not forget to be just, and fulfil their needs with this'". Sayyidina Zayd (RadiyAllahu Anhu) further says, when two or three days were left for the time to collect the dates, Sayyidina Rasulullah ﷺ (Salla lahu alayhi wa'ale hi Wasallam) was sitting near a well while returning from a funeral with the Sahaabah (RadiyAllahu Anhumma), among whom were Sayyidina Abu Bakr Siddique (RadiyAllahu Anhu), Sayyidina Umar Ibn Khattab (RadiyAllahu Anhu) and Sayyidina Uthmaan Ibn Affan (RadiyAllahu Anhu). "I came and caught the hem of the blessed shirt of Sayyidina Rasulullah ﷺ (Salla lahu alayhi wa'ale hi Wasallam) and cynically said: 'O Muhammad ﷺ, you do not want to pay my debt. I swear by Allah, that I know all the children of 'Abdul Muttalib' very well. You are very poor payers'.

Sayyidina Umar Ibn Khattab (RadiyAllahu Anhu) looked at me in anger and said: 'O enemy of Allah! what are you mumbling? I swear by Allah, that if I did not fear (the presence of Sayyidina Rasulullah ﷺ (Salla lahu alayhi wa'ale hi Wasallam)), I would have severed your head'. Sayyidina Rasulullah ﷺ (Salla lahu alayhi wa'ale hi Wasallam) was looking at me very calmly, and said smilingly to Sayyidina Umar (RadiyAllahu Anhu): "Umar, This person and I are in need of something more. He should have told me to take care in fulfilling his rights and should have advised in a better manner when putting forward his claim. Go, take him and fulfil his rights, and for having scared him, give him in lieu twenty saa' (approximately 66.5 kg) dates extra in excess of his right'.

Sayyidina Umar Ibn Khattab (RadiyAllahu Anhu) took me and fulfilled my rights and gave me the twenty extra saa. I asked: 'For what are these twenty extra saa'? Sayyidina Umar Ibn Khattab (RadiyAllahu Anhu) replied: 'This is the command of Sayyidina Rasulullah ﷺ (Salla lahu alayhi wa'ale hi Wasallam)'. I asked: 'Umar do you know me'? Sayyidina Umar (RadiyAllahu Anhu) replied: 'No'. I said: 'I am 'Zayd Ibn Sa'nah''. He asked: 'The Allaamah (great learned) of the Jews'? I replied: 'I am that very person'. Sayyidina Umar Ibn Khattab (RadiyAllahu Anhu) said: 'Being a man of such calibre, why did you behave before Sayyidina Rasulullah ﷺ (Salla lahu alayhi wa'ale hi Wasallam) in such a manner'? I replied: 'Two signs from the signs of Prophethood were left, which I was not able to test. The first is the hilm (gentleness) of Sayyidina Rasulullah ﷺ (Salla lahu alayhi wa'ale hi Wasallam) supersedes his ﷺ anger. The second is that, his ﷺ tolerance increases the more one acts foolishly towards him ﷺ. Now I have tested these two also, therefore I make you witness to my acceptance of Islam. I give half of my wealth in charity (sadaqah) to the Ummah of Sayyidina Muhammad ﷺ (Salla lahu alayhi wa'ale hi Wasallam)''.

Thereafter he returned to the noble presence of Sayyidina Rasulullah ﷺ (Salla lahu alayhi wa'ale hi Wasallam) and accepted Islam. Later he took part in many battles and was martyred in the 'Battle of Tabuk' (May Allah be pleased with him). -

(Tirmidhi / Al Bayhaqi / At-Tabarani / Jam'u al Fawaa-id and Jam'ul Wasaa-il).

The Justice of the Messenger ﷺ of Allah

'But no, by your Lord, they can have no real faith until they make you judge in all disputes between them, and find in themselves no resistance against your decisions, and submit with the fullest submission'. (Al Qur'an; 4:65)

This above verse from the Noble Qur'an, has stated in no uncertain terms that the judgement of the Messenger ﷺ of Allah, is to be accepted as the Divine Order of Allah (SWT), and must not be opposed. This is a matter of our basic faith, and articles of belief.

Men who are just in all affairs, are respected, and even honoured by their adversaries. This is a quality, which is as rare as having patience or mercy. When a person becomes affluent, takes leadership of others, then to find him to be just, is even less common. Being just is a sign of having balance, and being steadfast on the path of the truth. In one particular hadith, it is mentioned that certain people will be under the 'Shade of Allah', in the Final Hour, when there will be no shade but His.

It has been narrated by Sayyidina Abu Hurayrah (RadiyAllahu Anhu) that the Messenger ﷺ of Allah said, "Seven people will be Shaded by Allah under His shade on the day when there will be no shade except His. They are: (1) a just ruler; (2) a young man who has been brought up in the worship of Allah; (3) a man whose heart is attached to the Masjid; (4) two persons who love each other only for Allah's Sake and they meet and part in Allah's cause only; (5) a man who refuses the call of a charming woman of noble birth for an illegal sexual intercourse with her and says: 'I am afraid of Allah'; (6) a person who practices charity so secretly that his left hand does not know what his right hand has given (i.e. nobody

knows how much he has given in charity); (7) a person who remembers Allah in seclusion and his eyes get flooded with tears."

(Sahih Bukhari)

So what can be said about the justice of Sayyidina Rasulullah ﷺ (Salla lahu alayhi wa'ale hi Wasallam). It has been established through the books of *Seerah* that even before the revelations came, and the people of Makka became aware that Sayyidina Muhammad ﷺ ibn Abdullah, is the 'Seal' of all Messengers, they would know him ﷺ as *'Al Ameen'*, and *'Al Saadiq'*. They would approach him ﷺ to resolve disputes, and would always accept his ﷺ judgement. In the pre-Islamic times, there was a dispute between the rival tribes when a part of the Kaaba in Makka was re-built. They were on the verge of bloodshed on who will be given the honour to place the *'Hajr-e-Aswad'*, the 'Black Stone', in the Eastern corner of the Blessed Kaaba. They decided that the next person who would enter the sanctuary of the Kaaba, would be asked to decide between them. A young person entered, who was the Messenger ﷺ, and they were all delighted, and agreed that judgement would be given to him ﷺ. The chief of the tribes agreed that there is not a fairer person in Makka then Sayyidina Muhammad ﷺ ibn Abdullah (Salla lahu alayhi wa'ale hi Wasallam).

The people of Makka would entrust him ﷺ with their valuable possessions, even ahead of their own family, such was their trust in the Messenger ﷺ of Allah. Even when they opposed his ﷺ message, and the Call of Allah (SWT), they did not doubt the truthfulness of the Messenger ﷺ of Allah. It has been included in books of *Seerah* that on the day of Badr, al-Akhnas ibn Shurayk met the fierce enemy of Islam, the vile; Abu Jahl. He asked him, 'Abu-l Hakam, there is no-one here to listen to what we say. Tell me about Muhammad ﷺ, whether Muhammad ﷺ speaks the truth, or does not'? Abu Jahl, whose actual name was, Abu-l Hakam, replied, 'By Allah, Muhammad ﷺ is a truthful man, and does not ever lie'. (Ash-Shifa)

The accounts of Islamic history mention that when Sayyidina Rasulullah ﷺ (Salla lahu alayhi wa'ale hi Wasallam), sent letters to numerous Kings, inviting them to accept Islam, one of these kings was Qaysar. In some narrations it is stated that he kissed the letter and put it on his head. He then covered it with silk and put it safely away. He sent for the Pope and discussed this matter with him. The Pope said: 'Verily this is the last of the Prophets, the good news of which has been mentioned in our Holy Books'. The Qaysar said: 'I also believe this, but there is one problem, if I become a Muslim these people will kill me, and I will lose my kingdom'.

(I'laamus Saa-i-leen)

During a journey, he came across a convoy from Makka. Among them was Abu Sufyan, who was an opponent of Islam at the time, but had entered into a treaty with the Messenger ﷺ of Allah, after the events of Hudaybiyah. Qaysar wished to meet Abu Sufyan, and ask him about the Messenger ﷺ of Allah. He invited Abu Sufyan, and asked his companions to stand behind him, and motion if he was not telling the truth. Abu Sufyan was asked about the religion that the Messenger ﷺ of Allah brought, and his ﷺ blessed lineage, his ﷺ followers, and also asked whether the Messenger ﷺ of Allah was ever accused of falsehood. Abu Sufyan replied, 'Never'.

(Ash'aam–il)

The authentic ahadith mention that the Messenger ﷺ of Allah was always known as a truthful man, further narrations are included below;

Sayyidina Ali ibn Abi Talib (Ra) mentions, 'the Messenger ﷺ of Allah was the most truthful of people'.

(Tirmidhi)

Sayyidina Abdullah Ibn Masud (Ra) said, 'The best conduct is that of the Messenger ﷺ of Allah'.

(Sahih Bukhari)

Sayyidina Aayeshaa Siddiqua (Ra) has narrated, 'His ﷺ blessed hand never touched a woman, over whom the Messenger ﷺ did not have rights'.

(Sahih Bukhari / Sahih Muslim)

It has been extensively explained by Imam Qadi Iyad (Rh), in his highly acclaimed work; 'Kitab'Ash-Shifa' that the judgements of the Messenger ﷺ of Allah between people were based on evidence, and rulings of Islamic law. The Messenger ﷺ of Allah received prophecies, which none after him ﷺ would ever receive. Therefore his ﷺ judgements were based on apparent testimonies; guidance of law; oath from those involved, as this enabled these judgements to become precedents for later people. These rulings formed his ﷺ *'Sunnah'* and the basis of Shariah.

The Perfect conduct of the Messenger ﷺ of Allah

The sign of a perfect person, would be known if they were perfectly balanced in all situations. Whether they were in public, or in private, whether they are in prosperity, or in poverty, if they are in happiness or grief, in security or affliction, with family, or with strangers, in leadership, or anonymity. If a person could remain perfectly balanced, then this would be a sign of perfection. Therefore only Sayyidina Rasulullah ﷺ (Salla lahu alayhi wa'ale hi Wasallam) was Bestowed perfect conduct in all aspects of life.

In this section, narrations are included on the manner which the Messenger ﷺ of Allah adopted with his ﷺ family members, children and with his ﷺ companions. There was never distance or pride in his ﷺ conduct, and as the blessed ahadith show, the Messenger ﷺ of Allah demonstrated good humour, but always remained truthful. Sayyidina Rasulullah ﷺ (Salla lahu alayhi wa'ale hi Wasallam) is a legislator, every action and his ﷺ every word became law. Therefore a ruling here on being humorous, is that it is permitted as long as you do not lie in doing so. The Messenger ﷺ of Allah always showed mercy to others, and this allowed his ﷺ companions whether young or old to approach him ﷺ and be comfortable in his ﷺ presence.

Sayyidina Abdullah ibn Haarith (RadiyAllahu Anhu) relates, "The laugh of Sayyidina Rasulullah ﷺ (Salla lahu alayhi wa'ale hi Wasallam) was but a smile."

(Ash'aam-il)

Sayyidina Abdullah ibn H̲aarit̲h̲ (RadiyAllahu Anhu) reports, "I did not see anyone who smiled more than Sayyidina Rasulullah ﷺ (Salla lahu alayhi wa'ale hi Wasallam)."

(Ash'aam-il)

Sayyidina Abu Hurayrah (RadiyAllahu Anhu) reports, "The Sahaabah (RadiyAllahu Anhum) asked, 'Ya Rasulullah ﷺ (Salla lahu alayhi wa'ale hi Wasallam) (O' Messenger of Allah), you joke with us'? Sayyidina Rasulullah ﷺ (Salla lahu alayhi wa'ale hi Wasallam) replied, 'Yes, I do not say but the truth."

(Tirmidhi)

Sayyidina Anas ibn Maalik (RadiyAllahu Anhu) relates that a person requested from Sayyidina Rasulullah ﷺ (Salla lahu alayhi wa'ale hi Wasallam) that he be given a conveyance. Sayyidina Rasulullah ﷺ (Salla lahu alayhi wa'ale hi Wasallam) replied, "A child of a camel shall be given to you". The person replied, "What shall I do with a child of a camel O' Messenger ﷺ of Allah"? (I want one for a conveyance). Sayyidina Rasulullah ﷺ (Salla lahu alayhi wa'ale hi Wasallam) replied, "Every camel is a child of a camel".

(Tirmidhi)

Sayyidina Shidad ibn al-Had (RadiyAllahu Anhu) reported: "The Messenger ﷺ of Allah, came out to us for one of the evening prayers and was carrying his ﷺ grandson Sayyidina Hussain ibn Ali (RadiyAllahu Anhu). The Messenger ﷺ of Allah came forward and put him down, then began the prayer with exaltation, and prayed. The Messenger ﷺ of Allah prostrated at the end of his ﷺ prayer for a long time. I raised my head and Sayyidina Hussain (Ra) was upon the blessed back of the Messenger ﷺ of Allah during prostration, so I returned to my prostration. When the Messenger ﷺ of Allah finished the prayer, people said, 'O Messenger ﷺ of Allah, you prostrated at the end of your prayer for a long time, until we thought something happened or you received a revelation.' The Messenger ﷺ of Allah replied, 'None of that happened. Rather, my grandson was riding on my back and I disliked to rush him before he met his needs.'"

(Sunan An-Nasā'ī)

Sayyidina Abu Hurayrah (RadiyAllahu Anhu) narrates from the Messenger ﷺ of Allah, 'The one who does not show kindness to the young, or respect the rights of the elders, is not one of us '.

(Sahih Bukhari)

The Messenger ﷺ of Allah used to play with children even in the streets while walking. Sayyidina Ya'la Ibn Mura (RadiyAllahu Anhu) says: "I went out with the Messenger ﷺ of Allah for a food invitation. Sayyidina Hussain ibn Ali (RadiyAllahu Anhu) was playing in the street, whereupon the Messenger ﷺ hurried in front of the people towards him to catch him while Imam Hussain (Ra) was running right and left to escape. Moreover, the Messenger ﷺ of Allah would take Sayyidina Osama Ibn Zaid and Sayyidina Hassan Ibn Ali, May Allah (SWT) Be Pleased with them, and place them on his ﷺ blessed thighs then would tightly hug them and say: "O Allah Have Mercy on them as I have mercy on them."

(Sahih Bukhari)

The Messenger ﷺ of Allah gave special attention to children in a community, which shunned them. It has been narrated that Sayyidina Sahl Ibn Sa'd (RadiyAllahu Anhu) says: "The Messenger ﷺ of Allah was in a gathering and had something to drink, there was a boy on his ﷺ right-side and elders on his ﷺ left. The Messenger ﷺ of Allah asked the young boy, 'Do you give me permission to give this to them?' The boy replied, 'No, by Allah, I wouldn't give my share from you to anyone'.

(Sahih Bukhari)

This narration relates to Islamic culture that if something is being shared in a gathering, then the person on the right-hand side has the next claim to it. This is why the Messenger ﷺ of Allah asked permission from the boy to begin with the elders, who were on the left side first. But the boy knowing the rank of the Messenger ﷺ of Allah would not give up his drink, which had just been tasted by the Messenger ﷺ of Allah.

Sayyidina Jabir ibn Abdullah (RadiyAllahu Anhu) narrates from the Messenger ﷺ of Allah, 'Whoever has three daughters, gives them shelter, meets all their needs, and shows them kindness, will surely find his ultimate abode in Al-Jannah'. A man asked from the gathering, 'If someone has two daughters'? The Messenger ﷺ of Allah replied, 'Two also'.

(Sahih Bukhari)

Sayyidina Jabir (RadiyAllahu Anhu) narrates that the Messenger ﷺ of Allah was pretending to be a camel, and his ﷺ blessed grandsons (RadiyAllahu Anhumma) were riding on his ﷺ blessed back. Sayyidina Rasulullah (Salla lahu alayhi wa'ale hi Wasallam) was walking on his ﷺ blessed hands and feet.

When Sayyidina Umar ibn Khattab (RadiyAllahu Anhu) saw this, and said, 'How wonderful is your ride'. The Messenger ﷺ of Allah, added, 'How wonderful the riders are'.

(Ibn Hajar)

Sayyidina Aayeshaa Siddiqua (RadiyAllahu Anha), *Umm-e-Mumineen*, narrates, while on a journey with the Messenger ﷺ of Allah, the Messenger ﷺ told the people to go ahead. She narrated 'When we were left behind far enough, the Messenger ﷺ told me, 'Let's race!'. I was thinner then and I had a race with the Messenger ﷺ, and I outstripped him ﷺ on my feet.
The Messenger ﷺ of Allah did not mention it again until I put on some weight. Meanwhile I completely forgot about this incident. During another journey, the Messenger ﷺ of Allah told the people to go ahead. When they went far away, the Messenger ﷺ said to me, "Let's race!" This time, the Messenger ﷺ of Allah beat me and started to laugh saying "we are even now."'

(Sunan Abu Daawud)

In a time when the inhuman traditions of the Arab culture was to bury their daughters alive, the Messenger ﷺ of Allah was blessed with four daughters. There are many narrations of how the Messenger ﷺ of Allah honoured his ﷺ blessed daughters.

It was the noble practice of Sayyidina Rasulullah ﷺ (Salla lahu alayhi wa'ale hi Wasallam) to visit the house of Sayyidina Fatima az'Zahra (RadiyAllahu Anha) last before departing from Medina Munnawwarah, and upon returning would visit the house of his ﷺ blessed daughter first. When Sayyidina Fatima az'Zahra (RadiyAllahu Anha) would visit the Messenger ﷺ of Allah, the Messenger ﷺ would rise and kiss her blessed forehead. Similarly when the Messenger ﷺ of Allah, would visit Sayyidina Fatima az'Zahra (RadiyAllahu Anha), she would also stand up and kiss the blessed forehead of the Messenger ﷺ of Allah.

(Tirmidhi)

Sayyidina Fatima az'Zahra (RadiyAllahu Anha), the blessed daughter of Sayyidina Rasulullah ﷺ (Salla lahu alayhi wa'ale hi Wasallam) and Sayyidina Khadijah t'ul Kubraa (RadiyAllahu Anha), has countless virtues none moreso than the fact that she was so beloved to Sayyidina Rasulullah ﷺ (Salla lahu alayhi wa'ale hi Wasallam). There are many ahaadith on the qualities of Sayyidina Fatima az'Zahra (RadiyAllahu Anha), including having the title of being the *'Leader of the Women of Paradise'*. The hadith is found in the collection of *'Sahih Bukhari'*, where Sayyidina Rasulullah ﷺ (Salla lahu alayhi wa'ale hi Wasallam) says; *"Fatima is the leader of the women of Paradise"*. Allah (SWT) Bestowed the name *'Zahra'* for Sayyidina Fatima az'Zahra (RadiyAllahu Anha) which means 'Light'.

Sayyidina Aayeshaa Siddiqua (RadiyAllahu Anha) narrated many ahadith on the similarities between Sayyidina Fatima az'Zahra (RadiyAllahu Anha) and her blessed father; Sayyidina Rasulullah ﷺ (Salla lahu alayhi wa'ale hi Wasallam). Sayyidina Fatima Az'Zahra (RadiyAllahu Anha) was most similar to Sayyidina Rasulullah ﷺ (Salla lahu alayhi wa'ale hi Wasallam) in looks, character, honesty and generosity. It has been narrated by Sayyidina Aayeshaa Siddiqua (RadiyAllahu Anha) that she had not seen anyone more superior than Sayyidina Fatima az'Zahra (RadiyAllahu Anha) except for the Messenger ﷺ of Allah, and also said that she has not seen anyone more truthful than Sayyidina Fatima az'Zahra (RadiyAllahu Anha) other than Sayyidina Rasulullah ﷺ (Salla lahu alayhi wa'ale hi Wasallam). The Messenger ﷺ of Allah, said about his ﷺ blessed daughter that, 'Fatima is part of me'. Upon the passing of Sayyidina Rasulullah ﷺ (Salla lahu alayhi wa'ale hi Wasallam), grief overcame Sayyidina Fatima az'Zahra (RadiyAllahu Anha) and she passed away just six months after.

In a narration, it is mentioned that Sayyidina Ayeshaa Siddiqua (RadiyAllahu Anha) asked Sayyidina Fatima az'Zahra (RadiyAllahu Anha) why she cried and then laughed when speaking to her blessed father; Sayyidina Rasulullah ﷺ (Salla lahu alayhi wa'ale hi Wasallam) secretly during his ﷺ final days. Sayyidina Fatima Az'Zahra (RadiyAllahu Anha) replied: "My father ﷺ informed me secretly of his ﷺ passing so I cried. Then my father ﷺ informed me secretly that I would be the first amongst the members of his ﷺ family to join him ﷺ, so I laughed"

(Sahih al-Bukhari, Sahih Muslim)

Sayyidina Anas ibn Maalik (RadiyAllahu Anhu) reports, "A resident of the wilderness whose name was Sayyidina Zaahir (ibn Hiraam Al-Ashja'ee) (RadiyAllahu Anhu), whenever he visited Sayyidina Rasulullah ﷺ (Salla lahu alayhi wa'ale hi Wasallam) he brought with him presents of the wilderness: vegetables etc, and presented it to Sayyidina Rasulullah ﷺ (Salla lahu alayhi wa'ale hi Wasallam). When he intended to leave Medina, Sayyidina Rasulullah ﷺ (Salla lahu alayhi wa'ale hi Wasallam) used to present him with provisions of the city. Once Sayyidina Rasulullah ﷺ (Salla lahu alayhi wa'ale hi Wasallam) said, 'Zaahir is our wilderness, and we are his city'. Sayyidina Rasulullah ﷺ (Salla lahu alayhi wa'ale hi Wasallam) was attached to him. Sayyidina Zaahir (RadiyAllahu Anhu) was not very handsome.

Sayyidina Rasulullah ﷺ (Salla lahu alayhi wa'ale hi Wasallam) came to him once while he was standing in a place selling his merchandise. Sayyidina Rasulullah ﷺ (Salla lahu alayhi wa'ale hi Wasallam) embraced him from behind in such a manner that he (Sayyidina Zaahir (Ra)) could not see Sayyidina Rasulullah ﷺ (Salla lahu alayhi wa'ale hi Wasallam). Sayyidina Zaahir (RadiyAllahu Anhu) said, 'Who is this?'. However when he saw with the corner of his eye that it was Sayyidina Rasulullah ﷺ (Salla lahu alayhi wa'ale hi Wasallam), he straightened his back and began pressing it against the blessed chest of Sayyidina Rasulullah ﷺ (Salla lahu alayhi wa'ale hi Wasallam). (For as long as he gained this opportunity it was better than a thousand gifts). Sayyidina Rasulullah ﷺ (Salla lahu alayhi wa'ale hi Wasallam) then said, 'Who will purchase this slave'? Sayyidina Zaahir (Ra) replied, 'O' Rasul ﷺ of Allah (Salla lahu alayhi wa'ale hi Wasallam), if you shall sell me, you will be selling a defective thing, and will earn a very little sum'. Sayyidina Rasulullah ﷺ (Salla lahu alayhi wa'ale hi Wasallam) replied, 'No, you are not defective in the Sight of Allah (SWT), but much more valuable."

(Ash'aam-il Muhammidiyyah ﷺ)

The above narration shows the easy mannered conduct the Messenger ﷺ of Allah had with his ﷺ Companions (RadiyAllahu Anhumma). Sayyidina Zaahir (Ra) was aware that it was the Messenger ﷺ of Allah who was behind him but wished to enjoy the blessings of being embraced by him ﷺ. The Messenger ﷺ of Allah called Sayyidina Zaahir (Ra) a *'slave'* in humour, but it was still the truth as Sayyidina Zaahir (Ra) is a *slave* of Allah. Sayyidina Zaahir (Ra) would also joke with the Messenger ﷺ of Allah. For example, he would buy gifts and say that Sayyidina Rasulullah ﷺ (Salla lahu alayhi wa'ale hi Wasallam) would pay for them. Sayyidina Zaahir (RadiyAllahu Anhu) was not handsome therefore the Messenger ﷺ of Allah would give him special attention, saying 'But you are so worthy in front of Allah (SWT), so priceless'.

It has been related from Sayyidina Jarir (RadiyAllahu Anhu), 'Since I became a Muslim, it never happened that the Messenger ﷺ of Allah saw me without smiling at me. The Messenger ﷺ of Allah, once said, "Through this gate a man will enter, one of the best men of Yemen, whose face bears the touch of an angel". Then I came in'.

(Sahih Bukhari)

Sayyidina Jabir ibn Abdullah (RadiyAllahu Anhu), narrates from the Messenger ﷺ of Allah, 'Every good act is counted as charity, and a good act is to meet your brother with a smile, and to pour water from your bucket into his'.

(Sahih Bukhari)

Sayyidina Abu Hurayrah (RadiyAllahu Anhu) narrates from the Messenger ﷺ of Allah, 'When a person visits his sick brother, or just visits to enquire about him, Allah SWT says, 'May you be pleasing to him, May your journey be pleasant, and May you have a home in Al-Jannah'.

(Sahih Bukhari)

It has been related from Sayyidina Abu Barzah al-Aslami (RadiyAllahu Anhu), the Messenger ﷺ of Allah, said, 'Remove harmful objects from someone's path'.

(Sahih Bukhari)

Sayyidina Amrah (RadiyAllahu Anha) reports that someone asked Sayyidina Aayeshaa Siddiqua (RadiyAllahu Anha). "What was the usual practice of Sayyidina Rasulullah ﷺ (Salla lahu alayhi wa'ale hi Wasallam) at home"? Sayyidina Aayeshaa Siddiqua (RadiyAllahu Anha) replied: "Sayyidina Rasulullah ﷺ (Salla lahu alayhi wa'ale hi Wasallam) was a human from among other humans. Sayyidina Rasulullah ﷺ (Salla lahu alayhi wa'ale hi

Wasallam) himself removed the lice from his ﷺ blessed clothing, milked his ﷺ goats, and did all his ﷺ work himself".

(Tirmidhi)

The narrations below relate to treatment of servants;

Sayyidina Jabir ibn Abdullah (RadiyAllahu Anhu), narrates from the Messenger ﷺ of Allah in regards to the treatment of servants, 'Feed them with what you yourselves eat, provide them with clothes as you like to wear, and do not cause pain to any of Allah's Creation'.

(Sahih Bukhari)

Sayyidina Aayeshaa Siddiqua (RadiyAllahu Anha) reports: "Sayyidina Rasulullah ﷺ (Salla lahu alayhi wa'ale hi Wasallam) did not hit anything with his ﷺ blessed hands, besides the time when Sayyidina Rasulullah ﷺ (Salla lahu alayhi wa'ale hi Wasallam) made *jihaad* (Struggle / fought) in the Path of Allah (SWT). Sayyidina Rasulullah ﷺ (Salla lahu alayhi wa'ale hi Wasallam) did not hit a servant nor a woman (wife, slave girl etc.)".

(Ash'aam-il)

The Worship of the Messenger ﷺ of Allah

'Ta Ha. We have not sent down the Qur'an upon you in order for you to be distressed'.

(Al Qur'an; 20: 1-2)

The above verse was revealed at the time when the Messenger ﷺ of Allah would spend the entire night in prayer. The intensity of his ﷺ worship was such that the blessed feet of the Messenger ﷺ of Allah would become swollen.

The worship of a person is connected to their piety, their Awareness of Allah (SWT); and gratefulness. Therefore there can be no-one who could match the sincerity; intensity; and dedication in prayer of Sayyidina Rasulullah ﷺ (Salla lahu alayhi wa'ale hi Wasallam). The Messenger ﷺ of Allah has been narrated to have said; **'I have been made to love three things in this world of yours; women; scent; and the coolness of my eye is in the *Salaah*'. (An-Nasai / al-Hakim).**

The difference between the love of the Messenger ﷺ of Allah, and the love other people have for these things, is that the Messenger ﷺ of Allah loved them for the sake of their reward in the Hereafter. Also in this hadith, the Messenger ﷺ of Allah separated the love for scent and women, from the love of *Salaah* – prayer. As the love of prayer cannot be compared to the love of anything else in this world. This is especially true for Sayyidina Rasulullah ﷺ (Salla lahu alayhi wa'ale hi Wasallam), as in the Salaah, the Messenger ﷺ of Allah would witness the Countenance of the Lord, and have intimate conversation with Him. (Imam Qadi Iyad (Rh))

There are unlimited narrations in this regard, some are included below. Included here are also narrations relating to the fasting; and recitation of the Noble Qur'an, of the Messenger ﷺ of Allah ;

Praying

Sayyidina Ibn Abbaas (RadiyAllahu Anhu) reports: "Once Sayyidina Rasulullah ﷺ (Salla lahu alayhi wa'ale hi Wasallam) slept and began to snore. It was the blessed nature of Sayyidina Rasulullah ﷺ (Salla lahu alayhi wa'ale hi Wasallam) to snore, while sleeping. Sayyidina Bilaal (RadiyAllahu Anhu) gave the call to prepare for Salaah. Sayyidina Rasulullah ﷺ (Salla lahu alayhi wa'ale hi Wasallam) awakened and performed the Salaah. Sayyidina Rasulullah ﷺ (Salla lahu alayhi wa'ale hi Wasallam) did not perform the wudu (ablution)".

(Tirmidhi)

The above hadith is part of a comprehensive narration. This narration is also found in 'Sahih Bukhari'; and 'Sahih Muslim'. It is a peculiarity of the Ambiyaa – Prophets (Alayhimus Salaam) that their *wudu* – ablution does not become invalid by sleeping. For this reason, Sayyidina Rasulullah ﷺ (Salla lahu alayhi wa'ale hi Wasallam) did not perform wudu. Sayyidina Rasulullah ﷺ (Salla lahu alayhi wa'ale hi Wasallam) informed us of the reason, which is that when the Ambiyaa (Alayhimus Salaam) sleep, their hearts and minds do not sleep, only their eyes sleep. The dreams of the Ambiyaa (Alayhimus Salaam) are also Divine Revelations. (Tirmidhi).

Sayyidina Abu Hurayrah (RadiyAllahu Anhu) says: "Sayyidina Rasulullah ﷺ (Salla lahu alayhi wa'ale hi Wasallam) performed so many nawaafil (voluntary) prayers that his ﷺ blessed legs swelled

up. Someone said to Sayyidina Rasulullah ﷺ (Salla lahu alayhi wa'ale hi Wasallam): 'You take so many pains, whereas you have been given the good news that you are forgiven'. Sayyidina Rasulullah ﷺ (Salla lahu alayhi wa'ale hi Wasallam) replied: "Should I not be a grateful servant"?

(Ash'aam-il)

Sayyidina Aswad bin Yazeed (RadiyAllahu Anhu) says he enquired from Sayyidina Aayeshaa Siddiqua (RadiyAllahu Anha) regarding the Salaah (prayer) of Sayyidina Rasulullah ﷺ (Salla lahu alayhi wa'ale hi Wasallam) at night. Sayyidina Ayeshaa Siddiqua (RadiyAllahu Anha) replied: "Sayyidina Rasulullah ﷺ (Salla lahu alayhi wa'ale hi Wasallam) slept (after Isha prayer) for the first half portion of the night. Then Sayyidina Rasulullah ﷺ (Salla lahu alayhi wa'ale hi Wasallam) would wake up (and performed the tahajjud prayers) till the time of Suhur (dawn), thereafter Sayyidina Rasulullah ﷺ (Salla lahu alayhi wa'ale hi Wasallam) performed the Witr Salaah. Sayyidina Rasulullah ﷺ (Salla lahu alayhi wa'ale hi Wasallam) then went to bed. If Sayyidina Rasulullah ﷺ (Salla lahu alayhi wa'ale hi Wasallam) so desired, would go to his ﷺ blessed wife. Upon hearing the Adhaan (Call to Prayer), Sayyidina Rasulullah ﷺ (Salla lahu alayhi wa'ale hi Wasallam) got up. If being in a state of janaabah (requiring Ghusl) would perform ghusl (bath). If not, Sayyidina Rasulullah ﷺ (Salla lahu alayhi wa'ale hi Wasallam) performed wudu (ablution) and went for Salaah".

(Ash'aam-il)

Sayyidina Hudhayfah bin Al Yamaan (RadiyAllahu Anhu) says he performed Salaah with Sayyidina Rasulullah ﷺ (Salla lahu alayhi wa'ale hi Wasallam) one night. (It has been reported in a few narrations that this incident took place during a night of Ramadan. It is possible that this was 'tahajjud' or 'Taraweeh' salaah). After commencing the Salaah, this was recited:

Allahu Akbar, <u>dh</u>ul malakuti wal jabaruti wal kibri-yaa-i wal a-<u>z</u>a-mati
(Translation: Allah is Supreme! Lord of Dominion, Power, Majesty, and Magnificence.)

Sayyidina Rasulullah ﷺ (Salla lahu alayhi wa'ale hi Wasallam) then recited (after the 'Faati<u>h</u>ah') 'Surah Baqarah', and performed 'ruku' (bowing posture). The length of the 'ruku' was as long as the 'qiyaam' (standing posture).

Sayyidina Rasulullah ﷺ (Salla lahu alayhi wa'ale hi Wasallam) lifted his ﷺ blessed head from the 'ruku' and stood. This standing was also long like that of the 'ruku'.

Sayyidina Rasulullah ﷺ (Salla lahu alayhi wa'ale hi Wasallam) then performed the 'sajdah' (prostration). The sajdah was as long as the qawmah (standing in between the ruku' and sajdah).

Sayyidina Rasulullah ﷺ (Salla lahu alayhi wa'ale hi Wasallam) then sat up from the sajdah. This sitting was also long as that of the sajdah.

Sayyidina Rasulullah ﷺ (Salla lahu alayhi wa'ale hi Wasallam) recited in this salaah; 'Surah Baqarah', 'Surah Aali 'Imraan', 'Surah Nisaa', 'Surah Maa-idah' or 'Surah An'aam'. The narrator (Sayyidina <u>Sh</u>u'ba (RadiyAllahu Anhu)) is in doubt regarding the last two surahs, whether it is; Maa-idah or An'aam.

(Ash'aam-il)

The above hadith is part of a longer narration, but has been included here in a shorter version.

Sayyidina Abdullah bin Mas'ud (RadiyAllahu Anhu) reports: "Once at night, I performed Salaah with Sayyidina Rasulullah ﷺ (Salla lahu alayhi wa'ale hi Wasallam). Sayyidina Rasulullah ﷺ (Salla lahu alayhi wa'ale hi Wasallam) stood for such a long time that I intended to commit an evil deed". Someone asked him what deed did you intend to commit? He replied. "To sit down and leave Sayyidina Rasulullah ﷺ (Salla lahu alayhi wa'ale hi Wasallam) alone".

(Tirmidhi)

Sayyidina Aa-sim bin Damrah (RadiyAllahu Anhu) says: "We asked Sayyidina Ali ibn Abi Talib (RadiyAllahu Anhu) about the nawaafil that Sayyidina Rasulullah ﷺ (Salla lahu alayhi wa'ale hi Wasallam) performed in the day". Sayyidina Ali ibn Abi Talib (RadiyAllahu Anhu) replied: "You do not have the strength to perform these".

(Tirmidhi)

The commentary on this hadith mentions that Sayyidina Ali ibn Abi Talib (RadiyAllahu Anhu) referred to the level of dedication; humility; and steadfastness with which Sayyidina Rasulullah ﷺ (Salla lahu alayhi wa'ale hi Wasallam) performed these voluntary prayers, which could not be matched by anyone else.

Sayyidina Abdullah bin Saa-ib (RadiyAllahu Anhu) reports: "Sayyidina Rasulullah ﷺ (Salla lahu alayhi wa'ale hi Wasallam)

performed four rak'ahs after 'zawaal' before the 'Zuhr' salaah, and used to say: 'The doors of the heavens open at this moment. I like that a good deed of mine ascend there at this moment'".

(Tirmidhi)

Sayyidina Awf bin Maalik (RadiyAllahu Anhu) says: "I spent a night with Sayyidina Rasulullah ﷺ (Salla lahu alayhi wa'ale hi Wasallam). Sayyidina Rasulullah ﷺ (Salla lahu alayhi wa'ale hi Wasallam) used the 'miswaak' (cleaned his ﷺ blessed teeth), then performed the 'wudhu', then stood up in 'Salaah'. I stood with him ﷺ (joined him ﷺ). Sayyidina Rasulullah ﷺ (Salla lahu alayhi wa'ale hi Wasallam) began reciting, 'Surah Baqarah'. Whenever Sayyidina Rasulullah ﷺ (Salla lahu alayhi wa'ale hi Wasallam) came across an aayah (verse) of mercy, Sayyidina Rasulullah ﷺ (Salla lahu alayhi wa'ale hi Wasallam) paused and beseeched Allah of His Mercy. In the same manner when Sayyidina Rasulullah ﷺ (Salla lahu alayhi wa'ale hi Wasallam) came across an aayah of adhaab (punishment), Sayyidina Rasulullah ﷺ (Salla lahu alayhi wa'ale hi Wasallam) paused and beseeched Allah for His forgiveness. Then performed 'ruku', and remained in the ruku (bowing posture) for as long as Sayyidina Rasulullah ﷺ (Salla lahu alayhi wa'ale hi Wasallam) spent in the qiyaam (standing posture). Then recited in the ruku':

Sub<u>h</u>aana <u>dh</u>il jabaruti wal-malakuti wal-kibri-yaa-i wal-'a-<u>za</u>-mati

(Translation: Glory be to the Lord of the Might, the Dominion, the Majesty, and the Magnificence).

Thereafter, Sayyidina Rasulullah ﷺ (Salla lahu alayhi wa'ale hi Wasallam) performed the 'sujood' (prostration), which was as long as the 'ruku' and recited the same du'aa in the 'sujood' position. Sayyidina Rasulullah ﷺ (Salla lahu alayhi wa'ale hi Wasallam)

then recited 'Surah Aali Imraan' (in the second rakah), thereafter one Surah (in each rakah) and did the same".

(Tirmidhi)

Fasting

Sayyidina Anas (RadiyAllahu Anhu) reports: "Someone was asked about the Saum (fasting) of Sayyidina Rasulullah ﷺ (Salla lahu alayhi wa'ale hi Wasallam). He replied: 'It was the noble habit of Sayyidina Rasulullah ﷺ (Salla lahu alayhi wa'ale hi Wasallam) to fast on different occasions. In some months, Sayyidina Rasulullah ﷺ (Salla lahu alayhi wa'ale hi Wasallam) fasted for so many days, that it was thought Sayyidina Rasulullah ﷺ (Salla lahu alayhi wa'ale hi Wasallam) would continue fasting. In other months, Sayyidina Rasulullah ﷺ (Salla lahu alayhi wa'ale hi Wasallam) did not fast, we thought Sayyidina Rasulullah ﷺ (Salla lahu alayhi wa'ale hi Wasallam) would not fast now. It was also from his ﷺ noble habits that if one wanted to observe Sayyidina Rasulullah ﷺ (Salla lahu alayhi wa'ale hi Wasallam) perform Salaah at night, it was possible, and if one wanted to observe Sayyidina Rasulullah ﷺ (Salla lahu alayhi wa'ale hi Wasallam) sleep at night, this too was possible'".

(Tirmidhi)

This above narration mentions that the Messenger ﷺ of Allah would vary the amount of his ﷺ voluntary acts of worship, in order to avoid them becoming obligatory upon the Ummah. In regard to the compulsory acts of worship, the Messenger ﷺ of Allah demonstrated the steadfastness with which they have to be fulfilled.

Sayyidina Ummi Salamah (RadiyAllahu Anha) reports: "I did not observe Sayyidina Rasulullah ﷺ (Salla lahu alayhi wa'ale hi Wasallam) fast for two consecutive months, besides the month of 'Sha'baan' and 'Ramadaan'".

(Ash'aam-il)

Sayyidina Aayeshaa Siddiqua (RadiyAllahu Anha) reports: "Sayyidina Rasulullah ﷺ (Salla lahu alayhi wa'ale hi Wasallam) (often) gave importance to the fasting on Mondays and Thursdays".

(Tirmidhi)

This hadith is further explained by the narration below;

Sayyidina Abu Hurayrah (RadiyAllahu Anhu) says: "Sayyidina Rasulullah ﷺ (Salla lahu alayhi wa'ale hi Wasallam) said: 'Deeds are presented (before Allah Subhana hu wa ta'Aala) on Mondays and Thursdays. I desire that my deeds be presented whilst I am fasting'".

(Tirmidhi)

Sayyidina Alqamah (RadiyAllahu Anhu) relates: "I asked Sayyidina Aayeshaa Siddiqua (RadiyAllahu Anha): 'Did Sayyidina Rasulullah ﷺ (Salla lahu alayhi wa'ale hi Wasallam) fix a day for voluntary worship? Sayyidina Aayeshaa Siddiqua (RadiyAllahu Anha) replied: 'The practices of Sayyidina Rasulullah ﷺ (Salla lahu alayhi wa'ale hi Wasallam) were of a continuous nature. Who among you has the strength, which Sayyidina Rasulullah ﷺ (Salla lahu alayhi wa'ale hi Wasallam) had?' "

(Tirmidhi / Bukhari / Muslim)

Recitation of the Noble Qur'an

Sayyidina Ya'laa bin Mamlak (RadiyAllahu Anhu) says: "I asked Ummul Mu'mineen (mother of the believers); Sayyidina Ummi Salamah (RadiyAllahu Anha) about the recitation (of the Noble Qur'an) of Sayyidina Rasulullah ﷺ (Salla lahu alayhi wa'ale hi Wasallam). Sayyidina Ummi Salamah (RadiyAllahu Anha) replied: 'Sayyidina Rasulullah ﷺ (Salla lahu alayhi wa'ale hi Wasallam) recited every word separately and clearly'".

(Ash'aam-il)

Sayyidina Qataadah (RadiyAllahu Anhu) narrates that Allah (SWT) gave to every Prophet (Alayhi Salaam) that was sent, beautiful features and a beautiful voice. The Messenger ﷺ of Allah also had beautiful features and a beautiful voice. Sayyidina Rasulullah ﷺ (Salla lahu alayhi wa'ale hi Wasallam) did not recite in a melodious tone as singers do.

(Ash'aam-il)

Sayyidina Ibn Abbaas (RadiyAllahu Anhu) says: "Sayyidina Rasulullah ﷺ (Salla lahu alayhi wa'ale hi Wasallam) raised his ﷺ blessed voice only to the extent that it might have been possible that if reciting in the house, those in the courtyard might be able to listen".

(Ash'aam-il)

Sayyidina Abdullah bin Mas'ud (RadiyAllahu Anhu) says: "Sayyidina Rasulullah ﷺ (Salla lahu alayhi wa'ale hi Wasallam) once asked me to recite the Qur'an to him ﷺ. I said: "O Messenger ﷺ of Allah, should I recite it to you when it has been revealed to you'? Sayyidina Rasulullah ﷺ (Salla lahu alayhi wa'ale hi Wasallam) said: 'I love to hear it from another person". Thereupon I began reciting *'Surah Nisaa'* (which begins from the last quarter of the 4th juz). When I reached this aayah:

"But how (will it be with them) when We bring of every people a witness, and We bring thee (O Muhammed ﷺ) a witness against these?"-

(Al Qur'an; 4:41)

I saw tears flowing from the blessed eyes of Sayyidina Rasulullah ﷺ (Salla lahu alayhi wa'ale hi Wasallam)"

(Tirmidhi)

This blessed hadith established the *'Sunnah'* of the Messenger ﷺ of Allah, of listening to the recitation of the Noble Qur'an.

Hadith of Sayyidina Imam Hasan ibn Ali (As) from ibn Abi Hala

The hadith below has been included as a conclusion to this section on the Prophetic Character of Sayyidina Rasulullah ﷺ (Salla lahu alayhi wa'ale hi Wasallam). It has been regarded as one of the most detailed single hadith in describing the blessed characteristics of the Messenger ﷺ of Allah. In addition to this, it has also been narrated by the *'Ahl ul' Bayt'*, the blessed household of the Messenger ﷺ of Allah. The narrators include; Sayyidina Hasan ibn Ali (RadiyAllahu Anhu); Sayyidina Hussain ibn Ali (RadiyAllahu Anhu); and they received the narration from their blessed father; Sayyidina Ali ibn Abi Talib (RadiyAllahu Anhu). May Allah (SWT) Be Pleased with them, and with Sayyidina Fatima az' Zahra (RadiyAllahu Anha); the blessed daughter of Sayyidina Rasulullah ﷺ (Salla lahu alayhi wa'ale hi Wasallam), who is the blessed wife of Sayyidina Ali ibn Abi Talib, and the blessed mother of Sayyidina Hasan ibn Ali, and Sayyidina Hussain ibn Ali, the pillars of the blessed household.

Sayyidina Imaam Hasan ibn Ali (RadiyAllahu Anhu) reports that: 'I asked my (maternal) uncle; Hind bin Abi Haalah, who usually described particulars and conditions of Sayyidina Rasulullah ﷺ (Salla lahu alayhi wa'ale hi Wasallam). I was longing to hear something about it. On my asking, he described the blessed features of Sayyidina Rasulullah ﷺ (Salla lahu alayhi wa'ale hi Wasallam). He said:

'Sayyidina Rasulullah ﷺ (Salla lahu alayhi wa'ale hi Wasallam) was imposing and majestic, others also held him ﷺ in high esteem.

His ﷺ blessed face shone like the full moon. The Messenger ﷺ of Allah was taller than medium height, but not quite being tall (A miracle granted to the Messenger ﷺ of Allah was that among all people, the Messenger ﷺ would always seem the tallest). The blessed head of the Messenger ﷺ of Allah was large, and hair neither curly nor completely straight. His ﷺ blessed hair was parted, and did not reach below the earlobes. The Messenger ﷺ of Allah was fair skinned with a wide brow, with thick eyebrows with a narrow space between them. The Messenger ﷺ of Allah had a vein there that throbbed when the Messenger ﷺ became angry. The Messenger ﷺ of Allah had a long nose with a light that reflected from it, which some thought was part of his ﷺ blessed features.

The beard of the Messenger ﷺ was thick. His ﷺ eyes were black, and had firm cheeks, a wide mouth with white glittering teeth, which had gaps. The hair on the blessed chest of the Messenger ﷺ of Allah formed a fine line. The blessed neck of the Messenger ﷺ of Allah was like it was made of pure silver.

The blessed physique of the Messenger ﷺ of Allah was finely balanced. His ﷺ body was firm and strong. His ﷺ blessed chest and stomach were perfectly in line. His ﷺ chest was broad, and his ﷺ shoulders wide. His ﷺ calves were full. The Messenger ﷺ of Allah was luminous.

Between the neck and navel of the Messenger ﷺ of Allah, there was a line of hair but not on the rest of his ﷺ upper body. The Messenger ﷺ of Allah had hair on the forearms, shoulders, and upper chest. The Messenger ﷺ of Allah had thick wrists, wide palms, strong hands and feet. His ﷺ blessed fingers were long. The Messenger ﷺ of Allah had high in-steps, and his ﷺ blessed feet were so smooth that water ran off them.

When the Messenger ﷺ of Allah walked, it was though the Messenger ﷺ was descending from a high place. The Messenger ﷺ of Allah walked with dignity, and swiftly. When the Messenger ﷺ

of Allah addressed someone, it would be with their whole blessed body. The Messenger ﷺ of Allah lowered his ﷺ glance, and would be the first to speak with his ﷺ companions, and would be first to greet others.

The Messenger ﷺ of Allah was always in deep reflection, and would not rest, only speaking when necessary. The Messenger ﷺ of Allah would spend long periods of time in silence. His ﷺ words were concise but comprehensive.

The Messenger ﷺ of Allah had a mild temperament, not being harsh or cruel. The Messenger ﷺ of Allah valued gifts, regardless of how small. The Messenger ﷺ of Allah did not censure anything, nor criticize or over-praise food. The Messenger ﷺ of Allah did not get angry because of these things. The Messenger ﷺ of Allah did not worry about securing anything for himself, or get angry for himself, or ask for help for personal reasons.

When the Messenger ﷺ of Allah pointed it was with the whole hand. The Messenger ﷺ would be surprised and would turn his palm upside down. When the Messenger ﷺ of Allah talked, his ﷺ blessed habit was to hold his ﷺ right thumb in his ﷺ left hand. When the Messenger ﷺ of Allah became angry, the Messenger ﷺ would turn away, and when pleased, the Messenger ﷺ looked down. His ﷺ laughter was that of a smile, and his ﷺ blessed teeth would become visible'.

Sayyidina Imam Hasan ibn Ali (RadiyAllahu Anhu) says. 'I did not mention this hadith (due to some reason) to Sayyidina Imam Hussain (RadiyAllahu Anhu) (brother of Sayyidina Hasan (RadiyAllahu Anhu)), for some time. Then I once narrated it to him whereupon I found that he had heard it before me. Sayyidina Imam Hussain (Ra) had already asked ibn Abi Hala what I had asked. Sayyidina Imam Hussain had also asked our father

(Sayyidina Ali ibn Abi Talib (Ra)) about the manner in which the Messenger ﷺ of Allah entered and left the home.

Sayyidina Imam Hussain (RadiyAllahu Anhu) said: 'I asked my father regarding the manner in which Sayyidina Rasulullah ﷺ (Salla lahu alayhi wa'ale hi Wasallam) entered the house'?

Sayyidina Ali ibn Abi Talib (RadiyAllahu Anhu) replied: 'When the Messenger ﷺ of Allah entered the house, the Messenger ﷺ distributed his ﷺ time into three portions; One portion for Allah (SWT). (In devotion; performing Salaah etc.); One portion towards his ﷺ family (fulfilling their duties. i.e. enquiring about their welfare, speaking, laughing and spending time with them, etc.); And a portion for himself ﷺ.

Sayyidina Rasulullah ﷺ (Salla lahu alayhi wa'ale hi Wasallam) distributed his ﷺ own portion into two. One for himself ﷺ and one for the people. The time for the people would be for the common people, not for the elite. The Messenger ﷺ of Allah would prioritise them over himself ﷺ. In the part reserved for himself ﷺ, the Messenger ﷺ would allocate time for the people of merit, according to their excellence in religion.

The near ones among the Sahaabah (RadiyAllahu Anhum) came to visit him ﷺ. Through these Sahaabah (RadiyAllahu Anhum), the Messenger ﷺ of Allah conveyed messages to the people, not concealing anything from them.

Sayyidina Rasulullah ﷺ (Salla lahu alayhi wa'ale hi Wasallam) adopted this method, giving preference to the *'Ahl'ul-Fadl'* (i.e. people of 'ilm - *knowledge* and 'amal – *righteous action*). Sayyidina Rasulullah ﷺ (Salla lahu alayhi wa'ale hi Wasallam) distributed this time according to their religious *fadl* (betterment).

From among those who came, some had one requirement, some had two requirements and some had many requirements.

Sayyidina Rasulullah ﷺ (Salla lahu alayhi wa'ale hi Wasallam) fulfilled all their requirements, keeping them occupied in things that benefited them and the entire Ummah. When they asked Sayyidina Rasulullah ﷺ (Salla lahu alayhi wa'ale hi Wasallam) about religious matters, Sayyidina Rasulullah ﷺ (Salla lahu alayhi wa'ale hi Wasallam) replied to them in a manner that benefited them. Sayyidina Rasulullah ﷺ (Salla lahu alayhi wa'ale hi Wasallam) would say: 'Those that are present, should inform those that are not present regarding these beneficial and necessary matters'.

Sayyidina Rasulullah ﷺ (Salla lahu alayhi wa'ale hi Wasallam) would also say: *'Those people who for some reason (veil, distance, shyness or awe) cannot put forward their requirements, you should inform me about their requirements, because, that person who informs a king of the need of another, who is unable to put forward that need, Allah Ta'aala will keep that person steadfast on the day of qiyaamah (Day of Judgement)'.*

Only important and beneficial matters were discussed in the gathering of Sayyidina Rasulullah ﷺ (Salla lahu alayhi wa'ale hi Wasallam). Sayyidina Rasulullah ﷺ (Salla lahu alayhi wa'ale hi Wasallam) happily listened to these matters from the Sahaabah (RadiyAllahu Anhum). There were no wasteful or non-beneficial talks in his ﷺ assemblies'.

In the hadith of Sayyidina Sufyan ibn Wukay (Ra), it has been mentioned;

'The Sahaabah (Ra) came to the assemblies of Sayyidina Rasulullah ﷺ (Salla lahu alayhi wa'ale hi Wasallam) for their religious needs, they did not depart before 'tasting' something (by 'tasting', this may mean the acquiring of religious knowledge).

The Sahaabah (Ra) returned from the assemblies of the Messenger ﷺ of Allah as *'men of fiqh'*, as torch bearers of *hidayah* (guidance) and goodness. (They spread these teachings amongst others).

Sayyidina Imam Hussain (RadiyAllahu Anhu) says: 'I asked (my father) regarding the manner in which the Messenger ﷺ of Allah would be outside of the house'.

Sayyidina Ali ibn Abi Talib (Ra) replied: 'Sayyidina Rasulullah ﷺ (Salla lahu alayhi wa'ale hi Wasallam) controlled his ﷺ blessed tongue and only spoke that which was necessary. Sayyidina Rasulullah ﷺ (Salla lahu alayhi wa'ale hi Wasallam) did not waste time in useless conversations. Sayyidina Rasulullah ﷺ (Salla lahu alayhi wa'ale hi Wasallam) made those who came to visit him ﷺ, feel at home and did not make them feel scared or ill at ease. The Messenger ﷺ of Allah brought people together, and did not split them.

The Messenger ﷺ of Allah respected and honoured the respected ones of every nation and also chose a leader for them. Sayyidina Rasulullah ﷺ (Salla lahu alayhi wa'ale hi Wasallam) warned the people of Allah's (SWT) Punishment. Sayyidina Rasulullah ﷺ (Salla lahu alayhi wa'ale hi Wasallam) also protected himself ﷺ from troubling or harming people. Besides being cautious and commanding others to be cautious, Sayyidina Rasulullah ﷺ (Salla lahu alayhi wa'ale hi Wasallam) never lacked in courtesy towards others.

Sayyidina Rasulullah ﷺ (Salla lahu alayhi wa'ale hi Wasallam) was concerned for the affairs of his ﷺ companions, made himself ﷺ aware about the relationships between them and rectified their faults. Sayyidina Rasulullah ﷺ (Salla lahu alayhi wa'ale hi Wasallam) praised good deeds and encouraged them. Sayyidina Rasulullah ﷺ (Salla lahu alayhi wa'ale hi Wasallam) explained the harmful effects of bad things and removed and stopped these. Sayyidina Rasulullah ﷺ (Salla lahu alayhi wa'ale hi Wasallam) followed the middle path in all matters. *(Not saying one thing at times and at other times saying something else)*. Sayyidina Rasulullah ﷺ (Salla lahu alayhi wa'ale hi Wasallam) did not neglect the guiding of people, it is possible that some became unmindful of their religious duties, or exceeded in a matter resulting in them becoming disheartened. For everything there was a special arrangement. Sayyidina Rasulullah ﷺ (Salla lahu alayhi wa'ale hi Wasallam) did not fall back in the truth, nor exceeded the limits in this. The Messenger ﷺ of Allah was prepared for any eventuality, and managed his ﷺ own affairs, and did now allow his ﷺ debts to reach the point where others had to assist.

Those who attended his ﷺ gatherings were the best of people. The best person in the eyes of Sayyidina Rasulullah ﷺ (Salla lahu alayhi wa'ale hi Wasallam) was the one who wished everybody well. The one with the highest status in the eyes of Sayyidina Rasulullah ﷺ (Salla lahu alayhi wa'ale hi Wasallam) was that person who considered, comforted and helped the creation the most'.

Sayyidina Imam Hussain (RadiyAllahu Anhu) says: 'I then enquired from our father regarding the assemblies of Sayyidina Rasulullah ﷺ (Salla lahu alayhi wa'ale hi Wasallam)'. Sayyidina Ali ibn Abi Talib (RadiyAllahu Anhu) replied:

'The Messenger ﷺ of Allah, began and ended all the sittings with the _Dhikr_ (Remembrance) of Allah (Subhan hu Wa'ta Ala). When visiting a place, Sayyidina Rasulullah ﷺ (Salla lahu alayhi wa'ale hi Wasallam) would sit at the edge of the gathering or wherever there was a place, and did not reserve a special place for himself ﷺ, and forbade others to do so. Instructing them not to leap over peoples' heads and go ahead. It is a different matter, that wherever Sayyidina Rasulullah ﷺ (Salla lahu alayhi wa'ale hi Wasallam) sat, that place became the focal point of the gathering.

Sayyidina Rasulullah ﷺ (Salla lahu alayhi wa'ale hi Wasallam) fulfilled the rights of every person present. That means, whatever right was due in talking and showing happiness, was fulfilled by him ﷺ, so much so, that every person present would think that Sayyidina Rasulullah ﷺ (Salla lahu alayhi wa'ale hi Wasallam) is honouring him the most.

The person that came to sit by Sayyidina Rasulullah ﷺ (Salla lahu alayhi wa'ale hi Wasallam) or came to him ﷺ for some purpose, Sayyidina Rasulullah ﷺ (Salla lahu alayhi wa'ale hi Wasallam) would remain seated till that person would begin to stand up. Whenever one asked Sayyidina Rasulullah ﷺ (Salla lahu alayhi wa'ale hi Wasallam) for something, that request was fulfilled kindly, and not refused. (If Sayyidina Rasulullah ﷺ (Salla lahu alayhi wa'ale hi Wasallam) did not possess the thing), a soft and humble answer would be given. The cheerfulness and pleasant manner of Sayyidina Rasulullah ﷺ (Salla lahu alayhi wa'ale hi Wasallam) was for everybody. Sayyidina Rasulullah ﷺ (Salla lahu alayhi wa'ale hi Wasallam) was like a father to them.

The whole creation was equal before Sayyidina Rasulullah ﷺ (Salla lahu alayhi wa'ale hi Wasallam) as far as rights were concerned.

The gatherings of Sayyidina Rasulullah ﷺ (Salla lahu alayhi wa'ale hi Wasallam) were the gatherings of; forbearance; modesty; patience; and trust. Voices were not raised therein, nor was anyone degraded or disgraced. If anyone committed a fault, it was not made known publicly. All were regarded as equals amongst themselves. (A person was not regarded according to his lineage or genealogy). The virtues of one over the other was according to the *taqwa* (piety) possessed. The small ones were loved. The needy were given preference. Strangers and travellers were cared for'.

Sayyidina Imam Hussain ibn Ali (RadiyAllahu Anhu) then asked his father how the Messenger ﷺ of Allah behaved with his ﷺ blessed companions. Sayyidina Ali ibn Abi Talib (RadiyAllahu Anhu) replied,

'The Messenger ﷺ of Allah was always cheerful, easy-mannered, and mild in nature. The Messenger ﷺ of Allah was never harsh, and did not shout or utter obscenities. The Messenger ﷺ of Allah did not find fault with others, nor over-praise people. The Messenger ﷺ of Allah abandoned three things for himself ﷺ; hypocrisy; storing up means; and anything that did not concern him ﷺ. The Messenger ﷺ of Allah abandoned three things in respect of others; censuring anyone; scolding them; asking about their secret affairs.

The Messenger ﷺ of Allah only spoke about things to seek the reward from Allah (SWT), in his ﷺ gatherings, the people would be so still as if there were birds sitting on their heads. When the Messenger ﷺ of Allah was silent, the companions (Ra) would talk among themselves, but did not quarrel in his ﷺ presence. When someone talked in the presence of the Messenger ﷺ of Allah, others remained silent. The Messenger ﷺ of Allah would laugh with them, and would express surprise to what they were surprised at. The Messenger ﷺ would remain patient with the travellers who would often be coarse in their speech. The Messenger ﷺ of Allah would say, 'When you find someone asking for something, then give it to him'. The Messenger ﷺ of Allah did not seek praise, except where necessary. The Messenger ﷺ did not interrupt anyone until that person had finished, or had left the gathering'.

Sayyidina Ali ibn Abi Talib (RadiyAllahu Anhu) has also narrated about the silence of the Messenger ﷺ of Allah;

'The Messenger ﷺ of Allah was silent for four reasons; forbearance; caution; appraisal; and reflection. The appraisal of the Messenger ﷺ of Allah, was in observing and listening to the people. The reflection of the Messenger ﷺ was on what would endure, and what would vanish. The forbearance of the Messenger ﷺ of Allah, was in his ﷺ patience. Nothing provocative angered the Messenger ﷺ of Allah.

The Messenger ﷺ of Allah would be cautious about four things; adopting something good, which would be followed; abandoning matters for others to abstain from; striving for what is beneficial; and establishing what would be good for the world and the hereafter'.

(Kitab' Ash-Shifa / Ash'aam-il Muhammidiyyah ﷺ)

PART IV – THE PROPHETIC REALITY

Introduction

Sayyidina Jubayr ibn Mut'im (RadiyAllahu Anhu) narrates: "Sayyidina Rasulullah ﷺ (Salla lahu alayhi wa'ale hi Wasallam) said: 'I have many names, I am Muhammad ﷺ, I am Ahmad ﷺ, I am Maahi ﷺ (the one who erases - eradicates) through whom Allah (SWT) has eradicated kufr (non-belief). I am Haashir ﷺ, whom Allah (SWT) will raise first on the day of qiyaamah, the whole ummah will be judged before my feet on the day of qiyaamah. I am Aaqib ﷺ (the one who comes last), and that 'Aaqib', after whom there shall be no other Prophet'".

(Ash'aam-il Muhammidiyyah ﷺ)

This final section is the core of this work, the preceding sections have highlighted briefly some of the attributes of Sayyidina Rasulullah ﷺ (Salla lahu alayhi wa'ale hi Wasallam), but they are by no means a reflection on the reality of the Messenger ﷺ of Allah.

In this section, there are verses from the Noble Qur'an, and narrations from authentic ahadith that support our basic beliefs that there can be no-one like the Messenger ﷺ of Allah. The attributes are only the 'signs', and the 'Muhammadan ﷺ Reality' cannot be comprehended through them. There are matters that have been veiled from the human intellect, and are only accessible by a select few who reach the heights of intimacy with the Creator. In terms of understanding the very essence of the Messenger ﷺ of Allah, this is beyond our capability. The night of *'Al Israa w'al Miraaj'*, in which Allah (SW) Unveiled the Knowledge of His Hidden Realms to His Beloved Messenger ﷺ, before conversing with His Beloved Prophet ﷺ; who is His Nearest Slave ﷺ, provided conclusive proofs that the reality of the Messenger ﷺ of Allah, is beyond that of apparent form.

In conclusion, presented below is a collection of verses from the Noble Qur'an, and authentic narrations, with scholarly findings on certain aspects of the magnificence of the Messenger ﷺ of Allah.

The Muhammadan ﷺ Reality

'There has come to you a Light from Allah, and a Manifest Book'

(Al' Qur'an; 5:15)

Below are examples of the understanding of great scholars of hadith, who have given their verdict on the meaning of 'Light' in this verse;

"It is the Prophet ﷺ (Allah bless him and give him peace)"   (Tafsir al-Jalalayn).

(Imam Jalal al-Din al-Suyuti (Rh))

"By Light, He means Muhammad ﷺ (Allah bless him and give him peace), through whom Allah has illuminated the truth, manifested Islam, and obliterated polytheism; since the Messenger ﷺ is a light for whoever seeks illumination from him ﷺ, which makes plain the truth" (Jami' al-Bayan).

(Imam Ibn Jarir al-Tabari (Rh))

Sayyidina Ibn Abbas (RadiyAllahu Anhu) has narrated that the 'Soul' of the Messenger ﷺ of Allah, was a light in the Hand of Allah (SWT) two thousand years before He Created Sayyidina Adam (Alayhi Salaam). That light glorified Allah (SWT), and the angels glorified by his ﷺ glorification. When Allah (SWT) Created Sayyidina Adam (Alayhi Salaam), that light was cast into his loins.   (Kitab'Ash-Shifa).

(Imam Qadi Iyad (Rh))

However, there is also no doubt that the blessed Messenger ﷺ of Allah was sent in the form of *'bashar'*, or 'human being'. This is essential to our core beliefs, and is part of our *aqeedah* – article of faith. But Allah (SWT) Gives the distinction that the Messenger ﷺ of Allah was sent in human form, yet is not like other men;

"Say: I am but a man like you who is divinely inspired that your god is but One God"

(Al' Qur'an; 18:110)

Similarly, in the verse below, Allah (SWT) also warns the believers that the Messenger ﷺ of Allah should not be treated in the same way, as we treat each other. Once again, this verse makes the matter clear that the Messenger ﷺ of Allah is a man, but not like others.

O you who believe! Raise not your voices above the voice of the Prophet ﷺ, nor speak aloud to him in talk as you speak aloud to one another, lest your deeds may be rendered fruitless while you perceive not.

(Al 'Qur'an; 49:2)

This matter can be understood further by the narration below. The Messenger ﷺ of Allah explained to the Sahaabah, May Allah (SWT) Be Pleased with them, they are not allowed to fast continuously, a practice that is called, 'Al Wisal'. This was only possible for the Messenger ﷺ of Allah, and no-one can be compared to him ﷺ.

The Messenger ﷺ of Allah said, 'My eyes sleep but my heart does not sleep'.

'I am not like you in any form. My Lord gives me food and drink at night'.

(Sahih Bukhari)

In the Noble Qur'an, Allah (SWT) Confirms;

'He does not speak of (his own) desire. It is only an inspiration that is inspired'.

(Al Qur'an; 53: 3-4)

The above verse revealed that the Messenger ﷺ of Allah only acted upon Divine Revelation, and inspiration.

Sayyidina Abdullah ibn Amr (RadiyAllahu Anhu) has narrated that he asked the Messenger ﷺ of Allah, 'Shall I write down all that I hear from you'. The Messenger ﷺ of Allah replied, 'Yes'. Sayyidina Abdullah ibn Amr (Ra) then asked, 'Both of when you are pleased and angry'? The Messenger ﷺ of Allah replied, 'Yes. I only ever speak the truth whatever my state'.

(Sunan Abu Daawud / Musnad Ahmed)

Based on the Qur'anic verses above, and the narrations, we conclude that the Messenger ﷺ of Allah must be followed in every matter, whether that of the religion or that of the world. The *'Sunnah'* of Sayyidina Rasulullah ﷺ (Salla lahu alayhi wa'ale hi Wasallam) is complete guidance without exception, and includes everything that was observed from him ﷺ.

'Whatsoever the Messenger gives you, take it. And whatsoever he forbids, abstain from it and keep your duty to Allah'

(Al Qur'an; 59:7)

The physical form of the Messenger ﷺ of Allah, was that of a human being. It would be afflicted by human conditions such as sleep; weakness; illness; hunger, yet these conditions could not affect the spiritual state of the Messenger ﷺ of Allah. The inward state of the Messenger ﷺ of Allah was not that of a human being, but of something far greater. This has been explained by Imam Qadi Iyad (Rahmatullah Alayh) below;

'The Prophets and Messengers are the medium between Allah (SWT) and His Creation. The Prophets of Allah, Peace be upon them all, convey His Commands; and Prohibitions; Warnings; and Threats. Their outward form are characterized by the qualities of men, and this is why they would suffer illnesses, and would have to pass away like other men. This physical form allowed them to convey the Message to their nations.

But the souls and inward characteristics of the Prophets of Allah, are associated with the Highest Assembly, and they possess those attributes that are similar to those of the angels, and are free of any possibility of alteration or error. If their bodies and outward form had been marked by heavenly attributes, the mortals would not have been able to receive guidance directly from them, live with them, and follow their path – *Sunnah*'.

(Imam Qadi Iyad (Rh))

The Presence of the Messenger ﷺ of Allah

'By your life, (O Messenger ﷺ), they are wandering about in their intoxication'.

(Al' Qur'an; 15:72)

In numerous places in the Noble Qur'an, Allah (SWT) has taken oath by the Messenger ﷺ of Allah. The above verse is an example of this. Allah (SWT) Would only take oath upon something that will endure, and does not cease to exist. This is referred to as; *'Hayaat un' Nabi ﷺ'*.

Sayyidina Abu Hurayrah (RadiyAllahu Anhu) reports that Sayyidina Rasulullah ﷺ (Salla lahu alayhi wa'ale hi Wasallam) said: "The one who sees me in one's dream, has actually seen me, because the devil cannot imitate my person".

(Ash'aam-il Muhammidiyyah ﷺ)

Sayyidina Abu Qataadah (RadiyAllahu Anhu) reports that Sayyidina Rasulullah ﷺ (Salla lahu alayhi wa'ale hi Wasallam) said: "Whosoever sees me, that is, in a dream, has seen that which is a fact".

(Ash'aam-il Muhammidiyyah ﷺ)

The above narrations relate to receiving the blessed vision of the Messenger ﷺ of Allah, in a dream. If this takes place then it is the actual vision of the Messenger ﷺ of Allah.

In the work of Imam al-Suyuti (Rahmatullah Alayh) the concept of the life of the Messenger ﷺ of Allah was explained. Imam Suyuti (Rh) is said to have been granted the vision of Sayyidina Rasulullah ﷺ (Salla lahu alayhi wa'ale hi Wasallam) over seventy-five times during the course of his life, while awake. This has been narrated by the great Jurist of the sub-continent; Mufti Muhammad Ameen (Rahmatullah Alayh) in his highly acclaimed book; 'Al Burhan – The Conclusive Proof'.

'We can conclude that the Prophet ﷺ is alive with his ﷺ body and spirit. The Messenger ﷺ of Allah remains in the same form today as when in this apparent world. Nothing has changed. However, the Messenger ﷺ of Allah has been hidden from our physical eyes, just as the angels are veiled from us, yet are alive. But whenever Allah (SWT) Wills to lift the Veils from the person whom He Wishes to Honour with the blessed vision of the Messenger ﷺ of Allah, that person will be Granted his ﷺ vision, seeing his ﷺ existing form'.

(Imam al-Suyuti. 'Tanwir al-Halak fi Imkan Ru'yah al-Nabi wa al-Malak')

AUTHOR'S NOTE

May Allah (SWT) Accept this effort. True is the Word of Allah (SWT), Perfect is the guidance revealed upon the pure form of the Messenger ﷺ of Allah.

Every effort has been taken to ensure accuracy during the completion of this work, however I am aware of my own shortcomings.

All Praise Belongs to Allah (SWT) for all the good you find within, only the mistakes are mine.

ALLAHUMMA SALLI' ALA SAYYIDINA MUHAMMADIN' ABDIKA WA RUSLIKAN-NABI- YIL- UMMIY, WA ALA' ALIHI WA SAHIBI WA SALLIM TASLIMAN BI QADRI' AZMATI DHATIKA FI KULLI WAQTIN WA HIN

(O ALLAH, BLESS OUR MASTER MUHAMMAD ﷺ (SALLA LAHU ALAYHI WA'ALE HI WASALLAM), YOUR SERVANT ﷺ AND MESSENGER ﷺ, THE UNLETTERED PROPHET ﷺ, AND HIS ﷺ FAMILY AND COMPANIONS, AND GRANT THEM PEACE, AS GREATLY AS THE GREATNESS OF YOUR BEING, AT EVERY MOMENT AND TIME).

Zulfiqar Amir Raja (23 July 2020)

REFERENCES

Al Burhan (The Conclusive Proof) – The Holy Miracles of the Soul and Spirit of the Universe.

(Mufti Muhammad Ameen (Rh))

Al-Muwahib al-ladunniyya bi al-minah al-Muhammadiyya ﷺ

(Shaykh Ahmad Shihab Al Deen Al Qastallani (Rh))

Kitaab ul' Shifa. (Kitab Ash-shifa bi ta'rif huquq al-Mustafa) - (Healing by the recognition of the Rights of the Chosen one).

(Imam Qadi Iyad (Rh))

Kitab Al Tanwir fi Isqat al-Tadbir

(Shaykh Ahmed ibn Muhammad ibn Ata'Allah al-Iskandari (Rh))

Miracles of the Holy Prophet ﷺ

(Imam Abul-Fida Isma'il Ibn Kathir (Rh))

Shama'il al-Habib ﷺ al-Mustafa ﷺ

(Sayyid Shaykh Muhammad al-Yaqoubi)

Stories of the Prophets – (Qasas al' Ambiya)

(Peace be upon them)

(Imam Abul-Fida Isma'il Ibn Kathir (Rh))

The Life of the Prophet Muhammad ﷺ: *Al-Siraay Al-Nabawiyya*

(Ibn Kathir (Rh))

The Nobility of the Messenger ﷺ of Allah: Ash-Shama'il Muhammadiyyah ﷺ

(Imam Tirmidhi (Rh)) (Zulfiqar Raja)

Included also are the authentic books of Ahadith;

Sahih Bukhari – **(Imam Bukhari (Rh))**
Sahih Muslim – **(Imam Muslim (Rh))**
Sunan Abu Daawud – **(Imam Abu Daawud (Rh))**
Musnad Ahmed – **(Imam Ahmed bin Hanbal (Rh))**
Sunan ibn Majah – **(Imam ibn Majah (Rh))**
Jaami Tirmidhi / Ashaam-il – **(Imam Tirmidhi (Rh))**

Sunan An-Nasai – **(Imam Nasai (Rh))**

(Rh) – *Rahmatullah Alayh*

A detailed synopsis can be found below for the two works of literature that were extensively used for this book;

'Kitab Ash-Shifa bi ta'rif huquq al-Mustafa'

Kitab Ash-Shifa bi ta'rif huquq al-Mustafa, (Healing by the recognition of the Rights of the Chosen One), of Qadi 'Iyad (d. 544H/1149CE) is perhaps the most frequently used and commented upon handbook in which the Prophet's ﷺ life, May Allah Bless him ﷺ and grant him ﷺ peace, his ﷺ qualities and his ﷺ miracles are described in every detail. Generally known by its short title, 'Ash-Shifa', this work was so highly admired throughout the Muslim world that it soon acquired a sanctity of its own for it is said: "If Ash-Shifa is found in a house, this house will not suffer any harm... when a sick person reads it or it is recited to him, Allah will restore his health." Ash-Shifa gathers together all that is necessary to acquaint the reader with the true stature of the Prophet ﷺ, may Allah Bless him ﷺ and Grant him ﷺ peace, with the esteem and respect which is due to him ﷺ, and with the verdict regarding anyone who does not fulfil what his ﷺ stature demands or who attempts to denigrate his ﷺ supreme status - even by as much as a nail paring.

(Source: Amazon)

'The Nobility of the Messenger of Allah: Ash-Shama'il Muhammadiyyah'

The classical text of **'Ash-Shama'il Muhammadiyyah'** has been the subject of hundreds of commentaries, and has been taught in many different languages around the world. Originally compiled by the great muhaddith; Imam Tirmidhi (Rh), the book comprises authentic and in-depth narrations on the characteristics and sublime qualities of Sayyidina Muhammad ur'Rasulullah ﷺ. The narrations outline the magnificent beauty of our Master; Sayyidina Rasulullah ﷺ along with insight into his unparalleled characteristics of kindness, humility, generosity and patience. 'The Nobility of the Messenger ﷺ of Allah' is the revised English edition of the 'Shama-il', with extensive additional commentary providing in-depth analysis of the many rulings derived from the Ahadith, as well as explaining the crucial matters of Aqeedah (fundamental beliefs) which should be reflected upon. This version is an essential guide for anyone who wishes to know the Final Messenger ﷺ upon whom Allah (SWT) Granted perfection of form, character and message.

A renowned Shaykh gave this word of advice when commentating on the need to study the 'Shama'il' of Imām al-Tirmidhī (Rh);

'We advise that the 'Shama'il' (Prophetic characteristics) be studied before the Sirah (Prophetic biography). When studying the events in the Prophet's ﷺ life, one must know his character to fully understand his conduct'.

(Source: Amazon)

YA SAYYIDI SERIES

'Ya Allah, through my service to Your beloved; Our Master; Sayyidina Muhammad ﷺ ur'Rasulullah (Salla lahu alayhi wa'ale hi Wasallam), may You cure the ailments of my heart'.

Zulfiqar Amir Raja

Perfect is the Word of Allah (SWT) revealed to the universe as 'Al Qur'an', and perfect is the example of His Beloved Messenger ﷺ who is the Seal of Prophethood and the Seal of all the Messengers; Sayyidina Rasulullah ﷺ (Salla lahu alayhi wa'ale hi Wasallam), upon whom Allah (SWT) and Everything in His Domain, sends blessings and peace.

I would like to dedicate this work to my parents, who I owe everything to, and also to my blessed Shaykh, who brought me closer to knowing the Messenger ﷺ of Allah, and whose teachings have inspired me to begin the 'Ya Sayyidi Series'.

'Ya Sayyidi Series' is a body of work intended to enlighten Muslims and Non-Muslims as to the tremendous rank of the Final Messenger; Sayyidina Muhammad ﷺ ur'Rasulullah (Salla lahu alayhi wa'ale hi Wasallam). I established 'Call to Prayer', in 2005, an Islamic web-based programme with the vision of guiding the youth towards the true understanding of Islam and to revive the Sunnah. This allowed me an opportunity to begin television work, and also begin authoring books. The 'Ya Sayyidi Series' is a collection of books based on spreading true knowledge of the Supreme Rank of Sayyidina Rasulullah ﷺ (Salla lahu alayhi wa'ale hi Wasallam). My intention is ultimately this work benefits me as much as others whom I pray can be guided through knowing the *'best of creation'*, the one whom Allah (SWT) has called *'the lamp that gives light'*. Allah (SWT) Cures us through the service we give to His most Beloved ﷺ and this is the basis of my faith.

Ameen

Zulfiqar Raja.

OTHER TITLES AVAILABLE;

The Nobility of the Messenger ﷺ of Allah: Ash-Shama'il Muhammadiyyah ﷺ

(Extensive commentary on the Shama'il of Sayyidina Rasulullah ﷺ)

The Ascent of Man: A Journey to Al Aqsa

(Exploring the legacy of the sacred land of Jerusalem, and why Muslims should visit 'Bayt al Maqdis')

Knowing the Messenger ﷺ of Allah

(Book of Seerah for Beginners)

For more information, please visit;

www.rasulallah.info

For any enquiries, mail;

calltoprayer@hotmail.com

Facebook: Footprints of the Messenger ﷺ

Printed in Great Britain
by Amazon